The High Maintenance

bítch

{OWNER'S MANUAL}

LORI PACCHIANO & RYAN PACCHIANO
WITH MICHELLE GOODMAN

SASQUATCH BOOKS
SEATTLE

*In memory of our grandmother Agnes Dean
and brother Tim Pacchiano.*

Lola, I love you.

Printed in China
Published by Sasquatch Books
Distributed by Publishers Group West
15 14 13 12 11 10 09 08 07 06   9 8 7 6 5 4 3 2 1

Cover design: Nina Barnett
Interior illustrations: Lori Pacchiano and Lex Gable

Library of Congress Cataloging-in-Publication Data is available.

ISBN 1-57061-480-6

Sasquatch Books
119 South Main Street, Suite 400 / Seattle, WA 98104 / (206) 467-4300
www.sasquatchbooks.com / custserv@sasquatchbooks.com

Contents

Acknowledgments

Thanks to the remarkable group of people who helped create this project: Michelle Goodman, Lex Gable, and to all at Sasquatch Books: especially Terence Maikels, Dana Youlin, Bill Quinby, Gary Luke, Nina Barnett, Gina Johnston, Karen Parkin, and Amy Smith Bell.

To our friends and family: Mary Jo and Jerry Sweeney, Scott Williams, Hogan, Henry, Lola, Tanner, Brandon Kindle, Daisy, Liberace, Rachelle and Audrey Pacchiano, The Deans, The Pacchiano Family NY, Great Dog Daycare, Three Dog Bakery Seattle.

Thank you to the media for covering our brand with enthusiasm: especially Claudia Kawczynska, *Pet Product News*, *Seattle Magazine*, April Pennington, Nancy Bartley, Eric Riddel, World of Wonder, Angela Rae Berg, Lizza Monet Morales, Bravo, Wendy Diamond (*Animal Fair*), Kathy Schultz, Lauren Halperin (*Paw Luxuries*), Karen Woods, Bobbie Thomas, *Modern Dog*, Bruce Shenitz (*Out*), The Silver Spoon, Melissa Lemer & Princess Kayla, Lorena Bendikas and Lola.

Thank you to all the celebrities who have enjoyed HMB products and especially to those who have been kind enough to be filmed with them.

Thanks to all HMBs, you know who you are.

Introduction

It's not about being a dog, it's about being a bitch

For many years Girl's Best Friend has been misidentified as Man's Best Friend. But secretly, the female canine has had more in common with her human counterpart all along, from her fine taste in rhinestone-studded collars and fur-lined pet carriers to her expensive shopping, dining, and jet-setting habits. As today's woman grows more and more successful and independent, Girl's Best Friend is fast becoming her favorite accessory, not to mention her most trusted companion and advisor. Not only will the friendship, love, and incessant grooming demands of your four-legged bitch enhance your life, but they will also help you further embrace your own inner bitch.

So the next time someone calls your four-legged diva a little bitch, take it as a compliment. Because she's your best friend, you can revel in this praise with her, confident that this special word signifies the dazzling beauty, staggering intelligence, world-class wit, and impeccable taste you share. Stand tall and wear the word "bitch" as a badge of honor. From now on, whenever you hear this exultant word, the two of you can take pride in all the enviable qualities you both possess.

The Secret Language of Girl's Best Friend

One of the first things you will notice about having a bitch in your life is all the new words that you will come across. As you read through the meanings of these new words below, take some time to turn to your little bitch and give her a kiss on the top of her head to thank her for your new vocabulary enhancement.

High Maintenance Bitch (HMB). Once referred to as a dog, your bitch has acquired a new persona that exudes confidence, beauty, and freedom. She has a difficult time relating to the restraints and limits of her ancestors but lives her life with hope and wild abandon. She loves fashion and faces her daily challenges with wit, humor, and confidence.

American Kennel Club (AKC). A national club that judges breed standards, equal to the scrutiny one might receive from a group of high school cheerleaders, only these cheerleaders are dressed in polyester suits. Although you do not have to be a purebred to be an HMB, you do have to be a purebred to run in this judgmental circle.

crate. A plastic cage used in early dog history as a method of stowing or imprisoning your bitch against her will. Although many dogs are still often locked in crates, this method is not recommended for the HMB, who prefers to be treated as an equal—in a more stylish space.

Girl's Best Friend. Though once considered a diamond, that has recently been replaced with your little bitch. Girl's Best Friend is a companion who is able and willing to accompany you everywhere while always there to offer emotional support. She is your "mini me," and her loyalty surpasses any friendship you have ever experienced.

moppets. Manipulators of punishment; otherwise defined as children under the age of ten.

No Dogs Allowed (NDA) establishments. Cruel businesses that do not recognize her "money" qualities or the amount of money you spend on her. In your ultimate goal to liberate her, we recommend you do not patronize these businesses—but if you *must*, this book offers ways to sneak her in.

Purebred Bad Girl. A girl or dog who embraces her authentic self and balances it with a little disapproving fun.

spaw. A retreat for girls and dogs to enjoy pedicures, manicures, facials, massages, and other forms of lavish escape.

Is She an HMB?

Take this multiple-choice quiz to see if your canine cohort is truly a High Maintenance Bitch.

1. She'd rather

a. Chew on shoes.

b. Shop for shoes.

2. She lives in a

a. Doghouse.

b. Penthouse.

3. She sleeps in a

a. Crate.

b. Cradle.

4. When you give her a command, she

a. Obeys every word you say.

b. Sometimes does as you say, sometimes doesn't. After all, she likes to think for herself.

5. She prefers

a. Chasing the tennis ball.

b. Accompanying you to your tennis lesson—and watching you chase the cute instructor.

6. To her, purses are for

a. Ripping apart with her bare teeth.

b. Riding in, so she doesn't have to get her delicate little paws dirty.

7. She likes to

a. Get into the trash.

b. Read trashy gossip magazines.

8. You'll often find her tied up

a. In the backyard.

b. At the beauty parlor.

9. When your boyfriend spends the night

a. You make your little bitch sleep on the floor.

b. You make him sleep on the floor.

10. Her idea of a square meal is

a. The dry kibble you pour into her plastic dish.

b. Two to three of the most expensive items on the room-service menu, eaten off the hotel china.

11. To tame her, you

a. Teach her to catch a Frisbee.

b. Stock up on beauty products to smooth down her frizzy hair.

12. If your landlord didn't allow pets, you'd have to

a. Send her packing. She'd have to get her own apartment.

b. Move immediately. Being apart from her is out of the question.

Her Score:

If she scored 9–12 Bs, she is a High Maintenance Bitch to the core.

If she scored 4–8 Bs, with your help and support she'll be embracing her inner bitch in no time.

If she scored fewer than 4 Bs, she needs rescuing. Rush her to the nearest beauty spaw, buy her some new sequined accessories, and make her start sleeping in your bed.

Disclaimer

The High Maintenance Bitch Owner's Manual offers plenty of fabulous tips for you and your best friend but is presented in the form of parody. Use caution when following any instruction in this book, and consult with your bitch's vet before giving her any medications, meals, or perms. High Maintenance Bitch shall not be held liable for any errors in content, or for any actions taken based on information provided here. High Maintenance Bitch shall also not be held responsible for any of the following: bad perms, dog bites, unplanned pregnancies, upset stomachs, shin splints, swimmer's itch, broken heels, large cell phone bills caused by reading this book to your friends, tax evasion for writing off tanning and lattes (for you and your little bitch), and law suits arising from impersonating service dogs and from false impersonations of celebrities and/or celebrity pets.

CHAPTER 1

Girl Meets Dog

Girl loves dog

It happens every day. You've heard of girls who find love through an ad in the paper, or who look for a little love from someone who's been locked up for a long time. Sometimes it happens when you least expect it. You walk out of the grocery store, your eyes meet, and the next thing you know, you have some company in your bed. Falling in love is only half the story as you and your little bitch realize how similar the two of you are. The magic is in the journey of blending your two worlds into one—that is, yours. And together you will define High Maintenance Bitch.

Sugar and Spike

When you first get your little bitch, life will seem like one big happy movie montage: the two of you strolling along the beach, then sipping champagne, then riding in a convertible with the wind in your fur. Friends will joke about how inseparable you are, and the lavish party invitations will start rolling in. As a pair, you'll be the toast of the town. It will all be so intoxicating.

Then suddenly, as you find yourself throwing out the third bra she's devoured that week, the honeymoon will come screeching to a halt. You'll realize, somewhat resentfully, that you've become her maid, cook, chauffer, and bodyguard. Sometimes the responsibility will seem too great, especially when you wake up late for work with barely enough time to curl your hair, only to remember that she still needs her morning stroll through the park and three-course breakfast cooked from scratch.

It's important to remember that this relationship will involve some give and take, and that you're not slaving over a hot stove to make her turkey-rice omelets each morning for nothing. In exchange for all your careful doting, she will show you an immeasurable amount of loyalty, appreciation, and love. Commit to giving her your all, and you'll become the center of her universe. She'll prance by your side through thick and thin, even if it means jumping in front of a moving bus to save your life.

Types of High Maintenance Bitches

No two High Maintenance Bitches are alike. Yet these distinct types of bitch stand out from the crowd.

Which one best describes yours?
Each is a lady unique on all fours.

Rich Bitch

You're not likely to meet a bitch with more expensive taste than this one. A Beverly Hills or Manhattan native, her favorite stores are Neiman Marcus and Saks Fifth Avenue. Her favorite hobbies are rolling in cash, sniffing for diamonds, lounging in limos, and digging holes on the golf course. Her favorite colors are green and gold. As long as she looks better than everyone else—including you—she's happy.

Spoiled Bitch

This is one bitch who's willing to beg if it means she'll get what she wants. Suffice it to say, the word "no" isn't in her vocabulary. She lives for the beauty spaw, exotic travel, and shopping sprees (but always bring a carrier along; she's known to shop until she drops). Buy her a shiny necklace and she'll love you forever—or at least until she wants something new. Her favorite color is pink, and she looks best in anything that sparkles.

Royal Bitch

This little bitch will surely rule your life. Her favorite spot in the castle is the royal throne you had custom-built for her. She's most comfortable in jeweled crowns and velvet capes, and her favorite color is deep purple. As governor of your kingdom, she will try to dominate any suitors of yours who try to usurp her reign. She certainly is not afraid to bare her teeth and growl. Roll out the red carpet for her and make way for the queen.

Preppy Bitch

This bitch could have been a poster child for the "me" generation of the 1980s. Nicknamed "Yappy Bitch," she drools over convertible BMWs, argyle socks, and anything with her initials monogrammed on it. Her favorite color combo is pink and lime green, and she likes to wear her collar turned up. You'll often find her prancing around with her nose in the air because her life is oh so perfect.

Jealous Bitch

This bitch wants what you have; she likes to share because that means she gets half of what's yours. Because she's never satisfied, she hogs the bed, binges on cookies, and hoards all your shoes. Ever territorial, she'll pick fights with any person or pooch who moves in on her prized possessions—you being her most prized possession of all. It's safe to say she has a bit of an insecurity issue. The more jealous she gets, the more of your shoes she'll destroy.

Dumb Bitch

A fun-loving gal, this pup pretends she's less intelligent than she really is. Dumb Bitch is actually one of the smartest bitches around, but by playing the airhead, she avoids confrontation and escapes punishment every time. The key to handling your Dumb Bitch is to let her be her bubbly, boisterous, cheerleading self (after all, her best friends are a pair of pom-poms) without allowing her to manipulate you.

Sexy Bitch

Sleek, alluring, and easy on the eyes, this bitch knows how to captivate a room with just one sultry glance. Extremely confident and independent, she is happiest donning nothing but her birthday suit (though she's not one to turn up her snout at a big diamond collar). Her favorite pastimes include writhing naked on your satin sheets or on a bearskin rug alongside a crackling fire. She looks great in red silk and will never turn down the chance to join you for some lingerie shopping.

Mail-Order Breeds

If you think the Internet's only good for finding designer handbags on sale and trolling for a Friday-night date, think again. Many a love connection between girl and canine has been made online, thanks to the countless dog shelters and rescue services with Web profiles of pups to adopt. It's OK to be picky as you scroll through the pooch photo gallery. You want a bitch with just the right height, weight, hair color, and temperament. You don't want her to be too big, wild, or furry. Instead you're looking for your right-hand girl, that trophy woof who will hang on your arm (not to mention your every word) at art openings, cocktail parties, and family reunions. Once you find Ms. Right, not only will your days of flying solo be over, but you'll also feel warm and fuzzy inside knowing you're giving her a better life than the one she was born into. One great mail-order Web site to try out is www. petfinder.com.

She's a Little Bit Country

Pound puppies aren't the only four-legged children who need a good home. There's also the purebred prisoner. After all, not all pups that come with papers are born with silver spoons in their muzzles. Many purebreds are poor backwoods girls raised in puppy mills, dreaming of being whisked away by a worldly girl with a great manicure. Without your coming to her rescue, all her days might consist of helping Pa herd sheep and watching Ma churn butter. And at night, while gathered around the campfire with her twenty-six brothers and sisters, she'd forever gaze longingly at the stars, hoping that someday she'll meet a nice sophisticated gal like you and get out of Dodge for good.

Spring Her from Puppy Jail

If you are rescuing her from the pound, she'll probably be more than happy to leave cell block number nine in the dust. If you're buying her from a breeder, though—and therefore separating her from her umpteen brothers and sisters—she may take a little more convincing. Either way, you first need to prove to the "warden" at the pet shelter or puppy mill that you're going to give her a good home.

Get Her Past the Puppy Warden

Do not tell the warden of your plans to spoil her rotten and buy her a patent-leather leash that matches your favorite handbag. The warden will not understand why you wish to do this with an "animal." Instead, say that you already bought a big, ugly plastic brown crate filled with wood chips for her to sleep in. Now you're talking their language. The warden may also grill you on your income, lifestyle, and intentions for your new pup, so be prepared to answer questions like these:

What do you do for a living?

Say that you work from your house (say "house," not "home"; see below for details) as a technical writer, Web designer, accountant, or any other profession that pays well and allows telecommuting.

Do you live in an apartment or a house?

Well, as you said, you work from your *house*. Often puppy wardens will ask for your address and even a copy of a utility bill as proof. If you live in an apartment, do not fret. Simply "borrow" an opened utility bill from a friend or relative who lives in a house and give that address.

Do you have a yard?

Whether it's true or not, say you have a big, fenced yard in a residential area and that you don't live near any busy streets. Bonus points if you live across the street from a big park.

Get Her to Nuzzle Up to You

If you're saving her from a puppy mill (but taking her from her first mommy), you're going to have to work a little harder to win her over. While the breeder is counting the money, take the old Gucci sweater you brought from home and rub it on the puppy's mama. If the breeder asks you what you are doing, tell him or her the mama looked cold. As you get into the car with your new baby bitch, you may be tempted to peel out of the driveway. Instead, keep your composure and smile serenely at the breeder. This is a good time to hold up your new pup and lift her paw in a happy little goodbye wave.

As you drive off, she may grow worried and scrunch her forehead into an adorable heap of wrinkles. Where are you taking her, she will wonder, and where is her mommy? Look at her lovingly and assure her that you are her new mommy. Put on the old sweater and she will soon worm her way into your lap. Hmmm, smells like old mommy but looks like new mommy.

Get Around a Pesky NDA Policy

Remember when you were in high school and snuck your boyfriend into your parents' house in the middle of the night? Remember the adrenaline rush you got as the two of you tiptoed through the house in the dark, afraid of getting caught? If you live in an apartment building with a No Dogs Allowed (NDA) policy, this is how you will feel as you smuggle your little bitch into the building.

Here are some tips for making sure the property manager doesn't catch you:

🐾 Use the emergency stairs and exits. Hide her in a handbag or duffle bag. Or wrap her in a blanket and pretend she's an actual baby. If your building is cat-friendly, stick her in a cat carrier before you make your way upstairs.

🐾 Make friends with the landlord or building manager and let it slip that you're not exactly a "dog person." Explain that you're allergic to them and pretty much grossed out by all the dirt and germs they track inside. You might even want to tell the building manager that you suspect your neighbor has a dog. That way, you can blame your bitch's barking on another tenant.

🐾 If your new dog is too big, you probably won't be able to hide her as you enter and exit the building. Instead, you'll have to come up with a good excuse for having her, like you're epileptic and she detects seizures (and you've got the forged doctor's note from a friend in med school to prove it), or you're in the witness protection program and she's your bodyguard . . . You get the idea.

If none of these tactics works, try bribing the building manager to keep quiet. Everyone has a weak spot, whether it's accepting monthly hush money, pricy bottles of scotch, or an all-expenses-paid trip to the Bahamas.

Introducing Your Roommutts

So you got a dog without telling your roommate. You're probably worried that she'll be mad you didn't consult her first, despite the fact that she didn't ask for your permission when her ex-boyfriend stayed over three nights last week. But more than her anger, you fear she will make you take your new dog back to the shelter or breeder.

Here are some ways you can coax your roommate into accepting your little bitch from the start:

- While on your way home, call her to say that you have a surprise. When you walk in the door, tell her that since it's the anniversary of you two moving in together you got the "household" a present to celebrate your friendship. When she reminds you that it's not your anniversary, say that it's your parents' wedding anniversary and you always get the two confused.

- Tell her your new baby German sheperd is a Chihuahua. This way she won't worry about how big your little bitch will get. When she starts sprouting like a weed, blame your roommate for feeding her too much. By the time your little bitch is full grown, your roommate will probably have come to love her.

- Pretend to name your little bitch after your roommate. No matter how your roommate feels about having a dog, she will be flattered by the gesture. Give your new pup a nickname, too (see page 12 for suggestions). This will secretly be her *real* name—the one you will use whenever your roommate isn't around.

- Take a digital picture of the two of them together. In a fancy font, add both their names above their heads (for example, "Jessica and Jessica"). Hang a copy on the fridge and put another in a frame next to your roommate's bed. The idea is to make her feel too guilty to ask you to return the dog.

E-mail the picture to all her friends and family. Let all the people close to her get excited about the dog, too. Seeing the two of them together will naturally make them think it's *her* dog. Be sure to remove the matching names from the photo; otherwise, everyone will wonder why she named her dog after herself.

Choose Her Showgrowl Name

When you pick up your new little bitch from the dog pound or breeder, she'll probably come with a temporary name like Freckles or Zipper. Give her a new name right away: This is your chance to reinvent her in your own image. Name her after a funny inanimate object (Stiletto, Olive) or your favorite designer shoe or handbag (Manolo, Gucci). But don't stop at her first name. Give her a full name you can register on her American Kennel Club (AKC) papers and shriek when you want her to know she's in trouble. This is what's known as her "showgrowl" name.

A good showgrowl name will sound a lot like a Kentucky Derby racehorse, such as Charlotte's Pumpkin Pie Princess. To pick out her showgrowl name, write it down, in the following order:

1. An adjective that suits her—for example, "Luscious," "Platinum," or "Flirty." (If you're stumped, use the color of your favorite nail polish or lip gloss.)

2. The name she came with ("Gretta," "Daisy") or the new first name you've decided to give her ("Chanel," "Prada").

3. An object you like—for example, "Tiara" or "Mercedes."

4. Another object, preferably one that's more feminine, such as "Flower," "Lady," or "Queenie" (bonus points if this word starts with the same letter as the word used in step 3).

String all four words together and you've got her showgrowl name: Dirty Dinah Diamond Diva, Naughty Maudie Mercedes Mistress, Pleather Heather Peacock Feather. . . . You get the idea.

Enjoy Dog-mopolitan Living

Just because you've fallen head over heels for your four-legged princess doesn't mean you have to roll over like a, um, dog if some of her belongings don't match your decor. Remember the time you shacked up with that boyfriend with the big brown eyesore of a La-Z-Boy? Just as you kicked his recliner to the curb, you can ditch her homely plaid puppy bed and prison-inmate dishes. This time the two of you will pick out her new home furnishings together. That way you can make sure she begins to develop your impeccable taste. Since the world looks like one big black-and-white photo to her, you'll want to pay particular attention to the color scheme she's drawn to.

Start by buying her a doggy feather bed, mini chaise longue, bone-china dish set, and high chair for the dining room. You can also get her a pint-sized body pillow and embroider her initials on it. And how about a coat rack for her leash, rain slicker, hat, feather boa, and harness? (Why should you be the only one who gets to hang up her wet clothes?) To make her feel more at home, you can fill the candy dishes on your coffee table with little treats for her. You can even make her a low wood box for the balcony—painted with a mural of a beach scene or sprinkled with glitter—and fill it with grass so she doesn't need to trot downstairs each time she has to go potty. Finally, don't forget to hang a mirror in the bedroom, low enough so she can admire her fabulous self in all her new clothes and accessories.

Host an "It's a Grrrl!" Puppy Shower

To celebrate bringing home your new baby bitch, it's imperative you throw her a puppy shower. Do not underestimate the importance of this event. It will set the stage for all her future social interactions with your girlfriends: Not only will she be making a first impression on them, but also you will be training them how to treat her. (You want them all to send her handwritten invitations to their martini parties and buy her Christmas presents, don't you?)

On the invitations, include a photo that shows her humanlike instincts. For instance, have her pose at a department-store cosmetic counter, or snap a shot of her licking the foam off a cappuccino in your favorite café. Once your girlfriends see she is one of them, they'll quickly accept her into the group.

At the shower, snap some glamour shots of her. Decorate her with the bows and ribbons from all her presents, and have her pose with each guest. These will make great photos for her thank-you notes. The importance of these pictures trumps any party games you might play or drinks you might serve. To guarantee these personalized photos make it to her guests' fridges and desks, touch them up on the computer by whitening her guests' teeth and smoothing out their forehead wrinkles. The more they love how they look standing next to her, the more they'll cherish this photo. Be sure to have her sign these notes with a pink paw print.

Note: *Let your girlfriends know that your apartment does not allow dogs and that the shower is for people only—no exceptions! This is your little bitch's day. She should not have to compete.*

CHAPTER 2

The Care and Feeding of Your Bitch

She's a real health mutt

By combining an active exercise routine with good medicine and finding the way to her heart through some home cooking, you will show your little bitch you care for her with these daily "I love you's."

Death by Chocolate

Human girls don't hold a monopoly on chocoholism. Your little bitch shares your sweet tooth and won't hesitate to sample that box of chocolates you accidentally leave on the coffee table. Unfortunately, chocolate contains theobromine, a substance toxic to pooches. Instead of metabolizing it quickly like we do, they can easily OD on it. The smaller she is and the more chocolaty confections she eats, the more dangerous it is for her. It can even be deadly.

Signs of chocolate poisoning in a pup include vomiting, diarrhea, agitation, excessive thirst, frequent peeing, irregular heartbeat, and rapid breathing; it can progress to seizures and even death. If you think she's gotten into some chocolate, call your vet or emergency pet clinic immediately. You can also contact the National Animal Poison Control Center at (888) 426-4435 or check out their Web site at www.napcc.aspca.org.

If your little girl is incorrigible when it comes to dessert pilfering, it may be wise to just banish chocolate from your home altogether. Next time you're having a holiday party or recovering from a derailed relationship, stick to butter cookies. She may get a tummy ache if she steals a few, but she won't risk her life.

Note: *In addition to chocolate, these ingredients are all toxic to her:*

- Raisins
- Onions
- Grapes
- Marijuana

Rex-ercise Regimen

She will always be excited to go for a run or walk with you. Not only will exercising together motivate you both to stay fit, but you will also save the small fortune you might have spent on an expensive gym membership or a personal trainer. For variations on the traditional run along the beach or stroll through the park, try these workouts.

She Likes to Be on Her Back

Enroll yourselves in a girls-only doggy yoga (or doga) class. Together you will become more limber and more serene, so much so that the class instructor will likely start referring to her as your little "dogi." Learning to slow down, breathe more deeply, and meditate together will also strengthen your bond. Buy her a comfortable leotard or a pair of leg warmers for the class. Make sure her ensemble matches your yoga pants and tank.

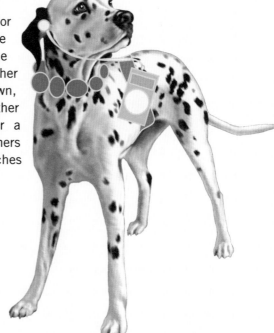

Lap It Up

She will love getting wet as much as you do, especially if you buy her a bikini that matches yours. Take her to a dog-friendly community pool or lake, or offer to housesit for your rich aunt with the backyard pool. To get your little bitch to follow you out to the deep end, simply call her name or entice her with a water toy. She also will be happy to join you for an evening skinny dip.

Keep in mind these health and safety tips:

- If you're bringing her to a lake, make her wear a floatation jacket.

- When playing in the sun, always have fresh water on hand (eight bowls a day) and a smidge of sunscreen for her snout.

- Be cautious of hot pavement—it will burn her paws.

- After swimming, clean out her ears with a vet-recommended ear cleaner.

Heart-Shaped Cookies

There is no better way to tell her how much you love her than a heart-shaped cookie.

Ingredients:
2 cups white flour
2 teaspoons baking powder
1 tablespoon honey
¼ cup vegetable oil
1 egg
½ cup skim milk
1 clove garlic, minced

Preheat oven to 350°F. Combine flour, baking powder, and honey in a bowl. Add oil, egg, milk, and garlic, then stir until mixed thoroughly, forming dough. Turn out dough onto a lightly floured surface and knead. Roll out the dough until it is ½-inch thick; cut with heart-shaped cookie cutters. Place cookies on a greased baking sheet. Bake for 15 minutes. Cool on a rack before serving. Store leftovers in an airtight container.

Give Her a Dip

The dog-training world is brimming with doggy dance classes you can take with her. Dog dancing—also called "canine freestyle"—is part obedience training, part agility training, and total fun. It's also as easy as walking her down the street. Whether you're learning the Chihuahua Cha Cha or the Terrier Tango, the two of you will have a ball as you spin around the dance hall. Practice your dance moves at home, too, so you can show them off to your family at weddings and holidays.

Sock Away the Moola
for Medical Emergencies

Just as you routinely need to get your roots dyed, she will need to get her shots, a new hairdo, and a pedicure every so often. None of these things will cost much more than getting your own nails done. But it's a good idea to have some extra dinero for those unexpected puppy emergencies, say if she swallows the squeaker from her favorite toy or falls off the end table and breaks her leg. (She probably won't have enough of her own cash to make her medical payments—even if you *are* giving her an allowance.)

Such veterinary emergencies often cost much more than getting your hair cut, straightened, and highlighted. In fact, upon getting the bill you may wonder if you could have bought yourself an extreme makeover for the same amount of cash. Some vets won't even help your pet until you've resolved how you'll pay for any necessary procedures. To better prepare for these medical mishaps, keep handy at least one credit card that isn't maxed out and a piggy bank stuffed with Andrew Jacksons.

Think of it this way: Imagine you give yourself first-degree burns with your curling iron and call 911, but the paramedics want to swipe your Visa card before treating you. If your card is maxed out, the scene would be reminiscent of the time you took your parents to dinner, only to realize that you'd left your wallet at home (on purpose). Dad paid for dinner and life went on, but can you imagine yourself lying on the stretcher, hearing one of the paramedics say your card has been declined?

Play Dog-tor

Whether she needs her yearly checkup or has indeed fallen off the end table, you'll want to make her veterinary visits as stress free and enjoyable as you can. To find a good vet near you, ask your dog-park friends, local pet-boutique owners, and your bitch's hair stylist for recommendations. The ideal veterinary clinic should smell of sweet candles, fresh-cut flowers, and home-baked cookies. The waiting and exam rooms should be clean and pretty. The floors should not resemble those of a hair salon.

Choose a Vet

When choosing a vet, make sure the clinic is right for her by phoning in and asking the receptionist these basic questions:

* *What does the office smell like?* (This will tip you off to how clean it is.) If it smells pine-scented fresh, she will tell you right off the bat; if not, she will dance around the question.

* *Why should I bring my dog there?* The receptionist should be more interested in the concerns you voice than treating you like another invoice.

* *Are there any hot, single veterinarians on staff?* Maybe you can get her a diagnosis and yourself a date all in one visit.

* *Does the vet have any celebrity clients?* This will make the waiting room visits more interesting.

Make Her Visit Painless

Before you head off for your veterinary excursion, tell your little girl you're taking her to a health spa. Do not use the words "vet" and "clinic." In case she has a horrible experience, you do not want her to associate these words with misery.

When you arrive at the vet's office, your bitch will immediately be intrigued by the delicious smells, yet she may be concerned by the muffled animal sounds coming from mysterious places. She also may want to meet the other clients in the waiting room, but try to dissuade her: You don't know who is contagious. To distract her, scoop her up in her favorite baby blanket, engage her in some baby talk, and give her a treat. If none of that takes her mind off her surroundings, some heavy petting may be in order.

When the receptionist whisks the two of you into a lilac-scented exam room, bring along a designer towel to place on the freezing-cold stainless steel table. Besides keeping your little bitch from catching a chill, this will prevent her little paws from slipping around. Have some baby wipes handy so you can disinfect the table first. And of course, lavish her with more treats for being such a good girl. Upon entering the room, the first thing the vet (or vet's assistant) will want to do is weigh her. If she has gained a few extra pounds, distract her with her favorite squeaky toy so she doesn't feel bad about herself.

Afterward, tell her she was a good girl and take her somewhere fun, like the mall or a dog-friendly martini bar. If the veterinarian is indeed sexy and single, leave your number for him at the front desk.

Remember, You're Driving the Ambulance

Let's hope you don't have to find out the hard way that dialing 911 won't help your little bitch in a medical emergency. If she has an accident that requires immediate medical attention, you will be the one driving the "ambulance." It's best to be prepared for a situation like this before it actually happens. Find out the location of the nearest twenty-four-hour veterinary clinic or hospital. Your regular vet can give you this information. Also, print the directions to the clinic and hang them on your fridge, which will be helpful for anyone babysitting your pet while you're out of town, too.

Fifi's First-Aid Essentials

Unfortunately, if your little bitch has a medical emergency, no handsome paramedic will come rushing to her aid—unless, of course, you are already dating a handsome paramedic who's willing to assist. Otherwise, you'll need to be prepared with the supplies and knowledge that will sustain her until you can get her the medical attention she needs.

To make a first-aid kit for her, fill an old makeup bag with these emergency essentials:

1. Syringes with the needles removed will help her to swallow liquid medicines. Turkey basters work well, too.

2. A thermometer so you can see if she's burning up (and K-Y jelly for when you have to surprise her in her hiney).

3. Contact lens solution for flushing foreign objects out of her eyes.

4. Iodine to disinfect minor cuts and scrapes.

5. A blanket that you can wrap her in if she is injured.

6. Gauze pads for bandaging or for pressure control if she is bleeding.

7. Scissors, tweezers, Q-tips, and adhesive tape for removing sharp or prickly objects from her soft little pads and legs, and cleaning out the wound afterward.

8. Medications that are right for your dog, such as children's aspirin for pain or allergy medications. (But check with your vet first and *never* use Tylenol; it is toxic for small dogs.)

She's Sick as a Dog

When she's feeling like dog doo, you can make her feel better by focusing all your attention on her. If you awake to find her under the weather, call in sick to work yourself. When telling your boss what's ailing you, describe the symptoms your little bitch is experiencing. Next, order your sick girl a bright bouquet of flowers. Open a window to allow fresh air in, too, but make sure she doesn't get cold. Put her on your bed or sofa if she isn't there already. Prop up her head on a lavender-scented spa pillow and cover her with a blanket. Here are some other ways to comfort her:

🐾 Sing to her.

🐾 Massage her head.

🐾 Stroke her ears and back.

🐾 Tell her jokes to make her laugh.

🐾 Turn the phone ringer off.

🐾 Cuddle up with her in front of the tube and watch Animal Planet.

🐾 Make her some white rice and boiled chicken breast.

🐾 Go online and order her a new collar. It will give her something to look forward to.

Pill Pupping

Getting her to take her medicine may not be the easiest task. If you try to pin her down, she will probably fuss and escape under the bed, and the pill will roll off and be lost forever. Her reaction will be much like yours when the lady at the makeup counter came at you with a blaringly bright blush that was all wrong for your skin tone and you had to turn your head before she could apply it.

To get your little bitch to take her meds like a good girl, try singing her this song while you prepare her pill. Make up whatever tune you want, or set the lyrics to your favorite electronica beat. She'll think you're playing a game.

Down your little pill
Little rock star girl
Flowers, stars, and vintage lace
This will put a smile on your pretty face

Now that she's distracted, roll a ball of butter just big enough to slip the mickey into. Make her sit before giving it to her so she thinks she's getting a treat. She will love the creamy taste as the ball slides down her hatch. Give her a kiss and consider her mutticated.

CHAPTER 3

She Doesn't Come Cheap

She tracks a cent

Your new little bitch really knows how to rack up a bill. Just like that friend you went to Vegas with during college. As you two eagerly dined with two older gentlemen you had just met, your friend kept ordering the most expensive wines on the menu—by the bottle. Each time another bottle appeared, you and your gentlemen companions looked at each other wondering, "Who is going to pay for that?" Today, your little bitch has replaced that other one, and you're the sugar mama who will have to fork over the dough.

Híre Her a Nanny

Finding a person to entrust your little bitch to when you're not home can be a harrowing process. Although a mother's intuition is powerful, you should thoroughly grill any puppy au pair you are considering hiring. Besides all the obvious requirements—reliable car; reasonable rates; good references; great hair, shoes, and a handbag you would die for—it's wise to hire an au pair who's multilingual. That way, your little bitch will have the opportunity to become fluent in more than one language. Bonus points if your new au pair is a gourmet chef and loves to shop at the same department stores as your little bitch.

Ask these questions as you sniff out a potential au pair:

1. Do you have a little bitch of your own? If so, what do you do with her during the day?

2. What other puppy-sitting experience do you have? Do you still sit for your prior clients? If not, why?

3. What do you like most about being a puppy au pair? What do you like least?

4. Can you work nights and weekends? How much notice would I need to give you?

5. What kinds of activities and games will you entertain my little bitch with?

6. What other languages do you speak?

7. Do you object to vacuuming, grocery shopping, and picking up my dry-cleaning while watching my bitch?

8. Do you cook? If so, what are your specialties?

9. Do you know CPR and other canine emergency procedures?

10. Do you take American Express?

After hiring a puppy au pair, invest in a nanny cam. If you witness the au pair doing any of the following, fire him or her immediately:

1. Trying on your lipstick and clothes.

2. Making long-distance calls.

3. Getting closer to your little bitch than you are.

Note: *You also can use your nanny cam to monitor how your new boyfriend treats your bitch when you're not in the room. If he isn't genuinely endearing to her, fire him, too.*

Gíve Her an Allowance

Oh, how the time will fly as you and your little diva enjoy a slew of sister-sister shopping sprees. However, you may start to notice her spending habits taking after, and possibly exceeding, yours. Soon she'll be giving you those big puppy-dog eyes every time she passes her favorite toy store or tries on a sweater at Neiman Marcus. Suddenly you'll find yourself struggling to pay your credit-card bills while she preens before the mirror in her latest purchase. Though the sassy little walk she does each time she comes home from the mall will be cute at first, her constant double-dipping into your joint checking account will grow old fast—especially once you realize she's more than happy to spend all your rent money on treats for herself.

The only antidote is to step out of the role of best friend and into the role of mother hen. You need to teach her some responsibility: To curb her spending, give her an allowance. A reasonable amount for this should be 12 percent of your income. You can either open a separate bank account for her or put her allotment in a puggy bank. You may even want to hold on to her debit card so she won't be tempted to use it. (You've already learned the hard way that every time you entrust her with it, she chews it up and you have to order her a new one.) If she really must have her own plastic, give her an old credit card you maxed out and swore you'd cut up but never did.

Get Your Sugar Daddy to Spoil Her, Too

Why should you be the only one getting wined, dined, and adorned with gifts by a sugar daddy? As you've undoubtedly learned, your little bitch loves a good spoiling as much as the next girl. And once your sugar daddy gets to know her better, he will come to lavish her with decadent treats, too.

Before we go over some tips on getting him to include her in his spending spree, let's take a moment to understand our subject, the sugar daddy. He is usually an executive or venture capitalist with good shoes, a nice car, a swanky mansion, and a penchant for wearing gold. Your sugar daddy is not your boyfriend, although he'd probably like to think he is. He usually has some sort of flaw (being fat, bald, or old) that prevents you from being attracted to him. In fact, you're probably on the market for a sexier, younger boyfriend, despite the fact that ol' moneybags keeps hanging around.

Getting your little bitch in on the gig should be no problem—any good sugar daddy knows that it's his job to pay for your friend. After all, he probably senses deep down that you aren't really comfortable being alone with him. Here are some ways you can get her in on your sugar daddy action:

🐾 Next time you're headed out for a shopping spree with him, tell him that you are bringing along a friend. Mention that she is cute and has an even better figure than you do.

🐾 Sugar daddies love to eat at classy NDA restaurants. You will never find your sugar daddy eating at the drive-thru unless you insist on it. It won't take more than one visit to the nearest McDonald's for him to buy you a new designer pup carrier that you can hide her in. That way, the next time he invites you to dinner, he can take you to his favorite NDA establishment.

Note: *When the three of you go out together, never leave him alone with her. You don't want to give them the opportunity to "cheat" on you. With your adorable canine vixen on his arm, he will receive an unacceptable amount of attention from other girls who may be in search of a sugar daddy of their own. You want to avoid this at all costs. (However, you shouldn't care whether he loves your little bitch more than you; in fact, that will take the pressure off you.)*

Work Her Like a Dog

There are times in every girl's life when the bills begin to pile up and the collectors keep the phone ringing off the hook. An eternity will seem to pass each time the grocery store clerk swipes your card and you, he, and the audience of people in line behind you wait to see if it will be accepted or declined. Even your canine counterpart will perk up her ears in anticipation, waiting for the receipt printer to make its series of clicks and beeps like a tiny choo choo train announcing to the crowd that you have been approved.

Instead, when that magical cacophony never comes, and you and your little bitch must make the walk of shame empty-handed past all the other shoppers with overstuffed wallets, you dream of the day when you get your Pretty Woman moment: You return to the supermarket and find the sales clerk who denied your card. "Big mistake! Huge!" you will tell him, waving a wad of cash in his face just before turning on your $400 heels and taking your business elsewhere.

During those lean times, your precious little one won't be able to help feeling like an added expense, especially when your cupboards run bare and the two of you are sharing rice and beans off the same paper plate each night. With a little creativity, though, you can become a two-income household. Your little team player will be more than happy to earn her keep. The possibilities of how you can pimp her out are endless. Here are our top-five suggestions:

1. Have her babysit a friend's dog.

2. Charge your brother by the hour to use her to get a date. She is sure to be a conversation starter on the walking trail and at happy hours downtown.

3. When the pooper-scooper guy makes his weekly pickup in your yard, tell him you've thought of a new business venture for him. Why should he let all that poop go to waste when he can turn another profit on it? Explain how, with a little hay and a composting bin, he can resell it as fertilizer. Once you have him nodding, tell him that with her droppings' suddenly inflated value, it wouldn't be right for you to let him pick it up for free. But tell him not to worry—your rate won't even be half of what he has been charging you.

4. Call a few of the big movie studios and ask if they are looking for a dog to be in any of their new films, even as an extra. If they ask what kind of experience she has in the industry, tell them she has tons. Create a portfolio you can bring to her interviews. Scan your fashion magazines and dog food cans for pictures of pooches that look like her. These will be her samples. This scheme also works for modeling agencies.

5. Teach her tricks like jumping through a hula hoop or leaping over you while you do somersaults. Put a whole routine together and perform at half-time shows, birthday parties, and bachelor parties. Wear matching outfits, of course. An old Wonder Woman costume found at a local thrift store is sure to land you some plumb gigs.

Write Her Off

Although she does depend on you for shelter, meals, medicine, and clothing, you might have a hard time claiming her as an actual dependent on your annual tax return. However, when April 15 rolls around, you still may be able to write her off as a business expense, especially if you work from home, run your own business, or are trying to break her into acting and modeling. Consider these pointers:

- Does she bark whenever she hears a noise outside? If you run a business from your home and rely on her as your alarm system, she could be a write-off.

- If you buy her with your company credit card and use her photo in your advertisements or on your client holiday cards, she could be a write-off.

- If you are a model and you do aerobics with her each morning, you may be able to write her off as part of your fitness-training budget.

- If you confide in her when you are having a bad day—essentially, if you consider her your therapist—she may be a mental health–related write-off.

- If you're trying to get her acting or modeling gigs, you technically are her agent. This means many expenses associated with trying to get her work "in the business" could be a write-off. When talking on your cell phone, for instance, make sure to end every call by asking if the person you're talking to needs her to do any modeling work. ("Hey, Mom, before you go, is there any modeling you need Lola to do, say, for Christmas cards or anything?") Now you can write off your cell phone bill, too.

Keep her receipts in your favorite shoebox and organize them into expense categories for your accountant: her exercise apparel, teeth whitener, monthly visits to the groomer, phone bills, airfare, hotels, room service, and so on.

CHAPTER 4

Give Her the Spaw Treatment

Paws and relax

Nothing will bring you and your little bitch closer than taking time

to reconnect to yourselves. With a little creativity you can provide

a chic environment in your home that will keep you both physically

and mentally balanced. She will love being pampered with all of your

Purebred Bad Girl beauty secrets.

Unleash Her Inner Beauty

What's the number-one beauty essential for your diva dog? Her mirror.

Every bitch needs a looking glass of her own. She spends so much time working out, shopping, and eating right, it's only fair she gets to enjoy her own dazzling reflection. It's pretty silly when you stop to think that she probably couldn't pick herself out of a police lineup. To rectify this situation, purchase a magnetic mirror like the kind you had in your high school locker and affix it to the fridge at her eye level.

When she gets her first mirror, she'll feel the way you felt when your mom bought you your first training bra. At first the experience will be incredibly personal. Then suddenly it will be the only thing she can talk about with her friends at the dog park. In time, though, batting her eyes at her reflection in the looking glass will become just another part of her daily routine.

Getting her a mirror is one of the nicest things you can do for her. When she first meets her new mirror, her reaction will be similar to that of a contestant on *The Swan*. (That is, once she realizes she's not looking at another dog and stops that awful barking.) At first she won't believe it's really her. She may take a moment and stare, puzzled yet intrigued. Then she may even take a couple steps back, put her little paws to her mouth, shed a tear, and gasp with unspeakable delight. As she twirls before the mirror, transfixed by her reflection, assure her, "Yes, it's you. You really are a beautiful little bitch."

Good Grooming

In the morning when you wake your pup,
before you put on your makeup
She'll ask a couple things of you . . .

She will most likely still be sleeping when you gently whisper "good morning" in her ear. Help get her ready for the day by making her look and feel fabulous. You wouldn't walk down the street with sleep goop in your eyes, dragon breath, or Medusa hair, and neither should she. All it takes is five minutes a morning to give her this quick touch-up:

1. Say "eye love you." With a warm, damp cloth, gently wipe her eyes clean.

2. Tell her "mother always nose best." Use the clean side of the cloth to wipe the surface of her nose.

3. Give her an earful. On a daily basis, moisten a washcloth or cotton ball with warm water and wipe out the insides of her ears. Once a week, clean her ears with a vet-recommended solution.

4. Paws for reflection. Apply a pet shea butter to her paw pads to smooth cracked, dry skin and wipe them clean with a cloth.

5. Tame her mane. Smooth down her tangled hair with a doggy brush.

6. Seal it with a kiss. Brush her teeth using a dog-friendly toothpaste and a children's toothbrush. Now she's more kissable.

How Sweet It Is to Be Bathed by You

You have always considered the bathtub your greatest escape, so why not take her with you? Bath time can be such a bonding experience for you and your little bitch.

The Setting

Here's how to create the perfect scrub-a-dub mood:

* Light some soothing scented candles and turn on some soft music.

* Fill the tub with warm water. Make sure it's not too hot.

* Turn off the jets in the tub if she's never been in a whirlpool. Her curiosity about the sound and the spray will distract her and make for a less-than-relaxing experience.

* Line the bottom of the tub with a towel or bathmat so she can sit comfortably without her paws sliding.

The Ingredients

What do you need for the perfect girl-dog bath? Girls and dogs can share a number of products found in luxury bath-supply stores. Dog products have a special pH balance that also suits humans. Try these:

* Bubbly bath soap. Be sure to put bubbles on her nose and blow them off.

- Shampoo that smells good. She's no dirty dog—she will enjoy bathing with you often if you clean her hair.

- Hair pudding. Get a conditioner that you can leave in her hair for several minutes. This will make her locks soft and luscious. Use a brush or comb to smooth the conditioner through her hair and remove any tangles. Rinse with lukewarm water.

- Bath fizzies or bon bons. Place a bath fizzy underneath her belly when she's in the tub. She will feel the tiny bubbles circulate all over her tummy like one of those $2,000 electric massage chairs you always see in airplane catalogs.

The Bath

Massage her ears and neck, and sing to her as you scrub her clean. Ask her how her day was and be sure to give her every little dirty detail of your day, as well. When the two of you have turned to raisins, help her out of the tub and dry her off with her own monogrammed towel. No matter how thoroughly you dry her, she still will want to shake the excess water from her fur. Her bath also may inspire her to run through the house like a bullet. Catch her and bring her to bed, tell her a bedtime story, cuddle up, and put a little lavender sachet under her pillowcase. She will have sweet dreams with you beside her.

Get Her a Doggy Doo

Maybe she's down in the dumps because you have been working a lot lately and it seems like you never take her out anymore. To lift her spirits, take her to the puppy salon to get a new doggy doo. A new look will put a smile on her face and a spring in her step. Here are some suggestions:

Haircut

You should have known better than to allow the girl with the straight, short Caesar bangs cut your own hair. It wasn't a total surprise, then, when she completed the cut and handed you the mirror—only for you to realize you both were now Julius look-alikes. In the same way, your little bitch is also at risk for a bad haircut. Whether you schedule her for a Supercut or a designer cut, bring pictures to assist the stylist. Scan all of your favorite tabloids to use as a guide for your little bitch's look. Is it layers you are looking for? Something coifed and sophisticated, the tossed salad look? It will be much easier for her stylist to craft the right doggy doo if he or she is able, for instance, to reflect on Nicole Richie's layers or Gwyneth Paltrow's bangs. And if your little bitch does have a run-in with Edward Scissorhands, do not tell her it's bad—tell her she looks amazing. She won't know the difference.

Perm

Do not give her a home perm. It's never the answer. Whenever friends give friends home perms, and they go bad, those perms can create broken friendships. Instead, call a friend who cuts hair at a swanky salon and ask her for a private after-hours appointment at the salon. Tell her the perm is a surprise for your best friend.

When you arrive, introduce your hairdresser pal to your little bitch and invite your bitch to take a seat in the barber's chair. Any hairdresser with a sense of humor will rise to the occasion and make your little bitch look ravishing. Be sure to give your hairdresser friend a big tip for being such a good sport. (FYI, before you book your bitch's appointment, check with her vet to see if the chemicals in the perm are safe.)

Highlights

This is one hair makeover for her you *can* try at home. Besides, it's the perfect way to celebrate summer. Next time you're mixing your home highlight solution, mix a little for your little bitch, too. Test a small lock of fur on her back to see how the color turns out and to see if there is an allergic reaction. Then give her a shimmering gold streak down the back of her head or neck. When people ask about it, tell them it's natural.

Extensions

She's never one to shy from the latest celebrity trend. The biggest stars are constantly going from shorthaired to longhaired, and so should she. Find a specialist who can work extension magic on your little bitch and watch as she's transformed from a Chihuahua to a collie.

Coloring

She's no ordinary girl, so she won't settle for the usual chestnut or strawberry-blond dye job. Instead, try dying her tresses pink, blue, green, purple, or a combination of all of these. You can get a kit to do this at home. Use a color chart to find the best color for her. Then dye her like an M&M.

Styling

You can change her style on a daily basis to match her mood or to suit whatever social engagement she's invited to, from barbecues on the beach to black-tie weddings. If she's going out for muttinis with you, give her sexy braids or cornrows. If she's going to the gym, give her ponytails. If you're taking her to see your favorite band, grab some hair gel and give her a mohawk or mullet.

Undercover Canine

Maybe she fell off her skateboard or she's still regretting that bitchy comment she made at the dog park. Who knew a bitch with a name like Fluffy could be so vicious? Now you find yourself examining the missing chunk of fur from her scalp. You don't want everyone to think she is aggressive, or worse, mangy.

To mask her cosmetic misfortune, use something distracting and glamorous—a flashy or glittery bright sticker will do the trick. Even better if it says something like "Good Girl" or "Angel." Or you can use some adhesive tape to stick on a sweet pink bow to camouflage her war wound. If her wound is still too fresh, try putting a tiara on her head to call attention away from her injury. Or if she has long hair, use some hair gel to create a comb-over even The Donald would envy. If worse comes to worst and someone detects her flaw, explain that a camera fell on her during a modeling shoot and that you are going to use the insurance claim money to have corrective surgery so it doesn't interfere with her work.

Quick Fix

Pay close attention to her nails. They double as her shoes. If neglected, her feet will click-clack against your floor like a pair of high heels. (Not good for your floors, and not good if you're trying to get some sleep.)

Most groomers will cut her nails for a reasonable fee. Schedule this service once or twice a month. Or if you want to use a doggy trimmer and trim her nails yourself, first try massaging her feet. If she is ticklish, she will pull them away. If so, you may have to restrain her. Your handbag works wonders in this situation. To create a harness to still your little bitch, turn your purse upside down. Place your bitch's head through the front strap and her legs through the back strap. Ask your roommate to hold the handbag upright. Your bitch will be surprisingly calm. Also, place her on a high surface like a countertop so it's easy to work on her.

Pay close attention to the quick of her nail. If you cut it accidentally, she'll bleed (and probably scream). If she has translucent nails, the quick will be easy to identify. If they are black, you will have to roll the dice and hope you get lucky. After you trim her nails, smooth them with a file and trim the fur underneath her paws so she has better traction.

When choosing a nail polish, go for canine polish. It is fast drying. This is helpful considering she may have trouble resisting the urge to put her foot in her mouth. She will love any color that matches what either you or she is wearing. She'll also love a French manicure.

She Picks Up a Scent

You spend so much of your time nuzzling her, you want to be sure she smells good. So take her to the perfume counter at your favorite department store. The two of you may differ on your scent preferences, of course. (For instance, she likes the smell of dirty socks, whereas you don't.) Keep the salesperson with the fragrance paper away from her. The power of your little bitch's nose is so strong she can probably smell the ladies' shoe department from where you are. Tell her that since you're the one with the credit card, you get to choose her scent.

Scent is one of her most important attributes, so use these suggestions to make a wise choice:

- Select something light and summery, like an herb garden or fresh-cut grass.

- Stay away from scents that a cheap whore might wear. Be willing to spend a lot of money so you both can wear her new perfume.

- If you live in a hot climate, find her a diluted fragrance. You don't want her scent to make people's eyes tear up.

- Try to find a perfume with the word "toilet" in the name. She likes anything with the word "toilet" in it.

Sign she likes her new smell:

She has a cute little spring in her step.

Sign she doesn't like it:

She throws up.

She's Begging for a Massage

Light a citrus aromatherapy candle or use similarly scented oil. (Remember, she has a much greater sense of smell than you. Therefore, be sparing with the aromatherapy.) Play some music that is soothing but energetic enough to wake her up.

1. Pretend you are going to pick her up like a Louis Vuitton bag and slide your hand back to her thighs.

2. Have her lay on her side and use your thumbs to massage the outside of the thigh that's facing up. Don't be afraid to use pressure; she will be the first to tell you if it's too much.

3. With your hand, squeeze the arm and leg facing up and gently pull from where her limbs meet her body to her paws.

4. Gently flip her to the other side so you can massage her other thigh as well as her entire arm and leg, as just described.

5. Massage her chest, concentrating on feeling her muscles and giving each one attention.

6. Massage her head and around her ears. Put your thumbs inside her ears, gently massaging and slightly pulling.

7. Work your hands around her jowls.

8. Gently wake her if she begins to snore.

CHAPTER 5

She Digs Holes, She Digs Fashion

Beauty is in the eye of the girl who beholds her

You are your little bitch's style maven. If she questions your fashion choices, tell her you are creating her image. She will soon trust you with blind faith. The key is to help her be a girl rather than to glamorize her dogness. Remember, she doesn't *know* she is a dog. She is fortunate to have a personal stylist. Remind her that usually only celebrities are privy to such services.

Fetching New Fashions for Girl's Best Friend

Your new little pup will look to you to pick the fashions that best suit her, which means you'll be outfitting her with a style that best suits *you*. This experience might remind you of the time you helped that friend of yours from middle school figure out what to wear the night of the big dance. She trusted you, and you came through for her. You remember telling her, "No, don't wear the pink dress. It's not a good color for you. Wear the black one; it brings out your eyes. Besides, I might wear the pink dress tonight."

Keep this experience in mind when shopping for your little pup. Don't worry— she is a team player. Of course her favorite carrier will be the one that matches your favorite shoes. And of course her favorite collar will be the one that matches your favorite handbag. She will want to exude all the qualities that you love about your favorite accessories. In fact, she may often compete to *be* your favorite accessory.

If ever you doubt whether she loves one of her new trimmings as much as you do, dig the receipt out of your purse and show it to her so she can see how much you spent on the shiny new item in question. The love you both share for expensive things will diffuse the situation. If that doesn't work, remind her that she is colorblind and that you know better.

Schedule a Clothing Consultation

Before you embark on a shopping spree with your little bitch, schedule a consultation with her. As her wardrobe advisor, keep in mind your primary objective: Are you trying to highlight her inner beauty, create a new image for her, or mask her Purebred Bad Girl behavior?

During your consultation, you will want to focus on her life "style"—the fashions that complement her hobbies and personality traits. If you're unsure of her style, here's an easy test you can give her to determine it: Place a platter containing a sausage, a cupcake, and last night's takeout on the floor. Watch what she chooses. Her taste should dictate her fashion choices, as her clothing will make a powerful statement about who she is.

Sausage: Hot off the Barbecue

She looks hot in a pair of extra high-cut Daisy Dukes. She loves gingham, beaded accessories, and sun visors. She may be a surfer girl, a jock, or an all-around outdoorsy girl. Her favorite holiday is the Fourth of July. Whether she's digging holes or disco dancing, dry-clean-only clothes are not suitable for this rustic little bitch.

Cupcake: She Wants You to Decorate Her Like a Cake

She is a delectable dessert and you are her confectioner. Bring out her sugary sweetness by combining chiffon, silk, cashmere, or any texture that is rich, smooth, and soft. Pinks, pastels, cherry red, and white are her favorite colors, and her favorite holiday to dress up for is Valentine's Day. Many of her clothes are dry-clean-only. Her clothing whispers, "Is she soft and sweet?" and seduces you with its look of virginity. She loves to wear anything frilly but not silly, demure but not pure, precocious but not preposterous.

Takeout: She's a Royal Red-Carpet Girl

Every day is an event to her. Feather boas and magnetic diamond earrings are her number-one accessory. She is a social butterfly who loves to party. Her favorite holiday to dress up for is New Year's Eve. She is willing to try anything you wear out. If you catch her chewing on a pair of your heels, she is most likely doing it because she's jealous that she can't learn to walk in them. She loves glitter and sparkles and textures that shimmer in the city night lights. She will beg for vinyl, leather, and steel, as well.

Don't Turn That Frown Upside Down

Have you ever noticed how runway models never smile? This is because clothing designers feel that smiling detracts from their creations. Therefore, if your little bitch hails from one of the frowning breeds (such as Boston terriers, Frenchies, English bulldogs, pugs, or Pekingese), they are more likely to wear their designer apparel better.

Note: *If she is seeking a career in modeling, be sure to use this point when negotiating jobs for her. If her breed is known for smiling, consider nude modeling instead.*

Take Her Measurements

Before you hit the mall, you'll need to know her size. Grab a tape measure and have her stand on all fours while you measure the following:

🐾 Collar size

🐾 Chest size

🐾 Distance from the nape of her neck to her tail

🐾 Height (determined by measuring from the top of her back to the ground)

Keep her measurements in a convenient place, such as taped to the back of your credit card. Whether you're buying off the rack or having her garments custom made, make sure to leave room for her to grow.

Fashion Before Function

If she's a harnessed girl, you can adorn her in necklaces and scarves since you are not relying on her collar to keep her in tow.

Collar for a Good Time

Her collar is her most important accessory. It is her staple, her little black dress. She should have several to choose from. Like a woman in her car, sometimes your little bitch will be judged by her collar alone.

She should always wear her collar: It says who she is and where she lives. Her collar is her swag—her business card. It should be sensible and durable, yet classy. With a cheap collar, you run the risk of making her look like a bathroom wall with her number scrawled on it. Choose a collar based on the image you are trying to create for her:

🐾 A diamond collar says she is spoiled and glamorous.

🐾 A pink collar says she is feminine and girly.

🐾 A black leather spiked collar says she is a tough girl who's not afraid to chew up all your stuff.

🐾 A red shiny vinyl collar says she's a bit of a rock star.

🐾 A polka-dot collar says she's into the 1950s Parisian look.

🐾 A webbed collar says she is an outdoorsy girl who likes to get dirty.

🐾 A bright neon collar says she's a beach bum who loves the sun.

🐾 A metal collar says she is very urbane.

Note: *Match her collar to your sports car. She will look good with her head hanging out the window.*

Harnessed for Adventure

Your vet once cast a disapproving look and said, "Only *spoiled* dogs wear harnesses." With that in mind, your bitch has worn harnesses ever since. Harnesses are the BMWs of pet discipline accessories. They handle better than collars, giving you more control over her. She will have a smoother walk, and so will you. If she's small and she misbehaves, you can hoist her in the air like Peter Pan. With collars, though, when she makes a bad choice and you pull her in the other direction, she chokes with embarrassment.

Imagine the two of you out walking through Manhattan. She's in the lead, so naturally she believes she's making the choices. Maybe she decides to take you to a little café on the Upper East Side. What a great time the two of you will have, she's thinking, when suddenly someone starts strangling her. She turns, surprised to see it's you. You literally drag her into a spendy boutique, as she's planted her little paws in the sidewalk, still coughing and wheezing from the struggle. If you want to get an idea of what she's feeling, attach one end of her leash to your neck and the other to hers. It won't take long to discover that the most civilized way to escort your canine companion is with a harness.

Escort Service

She likes to take the lead

The leash you choose to "hooker" up with should vary depending on the outing. Each time she sees you choosing a leash, she will be overcome with enthusiasm, anticipating the adventure to come. A leash represents your special connection with her, so be sure to invest in something unique and ultrastylish.

Her leashes should match at least one of the following:

🐾 Your heels

🐾 Your purse

🐾 Your lipstick

🐾 Her pet carrier

Keep a variety of leashes on hand for every occasion:

🐾 For formal events, choose satin, lace, or soft leather.

🐾 For playtime, choose plastic, vinyl, or a webbing with a fabric enhancement.

🐾 For shopping sprees, just make sure her leash matches her outfit—and yours.

🐾 For romps in the park, use a flowery leash. Flowers portray innocence and will help remind her to be a good girl.

🐾 For high-society shindigs or doggy daycare, invest in a custom leash. She'll be the envy of all the other bitches in her one-of-a-kind accessory.

She Gets Carried Away

Your little bitch will love to travel in style in her pet carrier, whether you're carting her around the city, traveling first class on an airplane, or smuggling her into a restaurant. Her carrier is like her mini mutt condo. In it, she's as secure and happy as a pearl in an oyster.

When choosing a carrier for her, consider both style *and* comfort. Will she be happier riding in a Ford Fiesta or a BMW? See if the carrier you're considering has a removable fur lining or cushion. And how about the window—does it offer a panoramic view or a small porthole? If she is more private, she might prefer the porthole. Does the carrier door or zipper have a safety latch or lock? Or is it simply secured with Velcro? If she's an escape artist, you may want to think twice about the Velcro. Before you buy, check how the carrier feels to you, too: Are the straps comfortable and functional, or do they dig into your shoulder?

Her carrier will be a great resting spot for her when she's partied too hard and is ready for bed. This way, you can tuck her in and order yourself another martini.

What to Where

When it's time to choose her look for the day, base the decision on her destination and always consider her comfort, style, and freedom. In the end, a real HMB will always care more about where she is going in life rather than what she is wearing, so it's up to you to dress her properly for each occasion.

Life's a Beach When You're a Surfer Bitch

She loves to spend her time by the "see" because everyone has their eyes on her. She'll want water-resistant, bright, flowery or striped fashions to wear to the beach, the pool, or even just the neighbor's patio for a barbecue. And a bikini is a must for this little bitch. Get her something sexy and flashy, maybe even a string bikini or thong. You can even make her a bikini yourself by cutting up a T-shirt and tying it on her. For winter, consider the cashmere bikini. It's soft and sexy, and it appeals to her swanky sensibilities.

Take Her with You for Muttinis

It always pays to have a friend who will flirt with the best-looking men and score free drinks. She is this friend. The heart-shaped blinker on her collar will create a mini disco-light show, much to the amusement of the other bar patrons. Add a metallic piece with retro appeal, possibly a halter or a headband that says, "Let's get physical." Her obvious sense of humor will make you more approachable. When men approach, tell them what she's drinking and to make it a double.

If it's a classy joint, dress her in a feather boa and some giant icy rocks around her neck to light up the room. Be sure to bring body glitter so when you girls head to the bathroom to freshen up she can get a touch-up, too.

Note: *To get a guy's attention, remove one of your bitch's magnetic earrings, drop it on the floor, and pretend to look for it. He'll think you've lost a contact lens or something. If he comes over to help you, ask if your bitch can buy him a drink as a thank-you.*

She Loves a Ball

Whether you're going to an Oscar party or "Customer Appreciation Day" at your favorite department store, this will be a beautiful evening of giant dresses and sipping bubbles. Some people may be surprised to see that she is accompanying you. As a service dog, she is able to escort you everywhere (wink). Hopefully tonight she will not have to detect one of "your seizures." Instead, the two of you and a prince charming will dance under the moonlight. Balls are like prom nights, and now that you have her you never need to miss one again for lack of a date.

Unlike the usual faux paw of wearing the same dress as another damsel, this time you *want* to match your bitch precisely. Find a seamstress who will work as your custom tailor. Provide her with your bitch's measurements, and she should be able to easily make her a dress that matches yours. Buy matching tiaras and necklaces, too. The portrait of the two of you will be priceless.

She Likes to Mosh

The off-leash dog park is one of her favorite places. Perhaps it's the unsolicited sexual advances she likes most. Or the fact that the attacks here are far worse than any bar fight. Or maybe she's attracted to the rampant drool, sweaty naked bodies, and strangers exchanging body fluids. It's like Studio 54 back in the day, only better.

When getting ready for the dog park, dress her in clothing that protects her from getting dirty; catching a disease; and being attacked, drooled on, and humped by strangers. When doing so, it is important to know her dog-park fetish. Is she a fighter? Then she should wear protective gear, like a big diamond necklace (fake, of course) in case another dog goes for her neck. Does she enjoy flirtatious humping? Then dress her in some frilly pants, something cute enough to allow her the pleasure of being a tease. If she's like the sweaty girl on the dance floor with everyone drooling on her, consider clothing her in something water resistant or disposable. The pup park is not the place to flex her fashion muscle—this is one of those very rare cases where she puts function before beauty.

Note: *When visiting the dog park, make sure she's fashionably healthy and has had all of her shots. Also, she should probably not be fertile unless she is looking for a surrogate.*

Tree Skirts and Other Holiday Attire

The holidays provide so many opportunities for you to show her off: work parties, family functions, cocktail gatherings with friends. No one likes to show up at a party alone; bring your little bitch along so she can help you shake it on the dance floor, watch your boss drink too much, and argue with your family about just what it is you're doing with your life.

Dressing her for the event is important, as there is always one relative, friend, or co-worker in the crowd who likes to enforce an NDA policy. For Thanksgiving, make a pet carrier out of a cornucopia. Attach two straps to the basket and carry her around in it. For Easter, dress her in bunny ears and carry her around in an

Easter basket. Let the other guests see that she is there for the party. If she's decked out in holly or flapping bat wings, it will be harder for anyone to ask her to leave, as doing so will take away from the party experience. Dressing her up will have everyone wanting to talk to the two of you.

Note: *While you two wait patiently under the mistletoe, make sure she does not eat any of it: It's poisonous and could be fatal. And if you catch her opening up someone else's presents, quickly shove the card in your pocket and tell any onlookers that it was a gift you got just for her. "She loves slippers" works every time.*

Use Her as a Decoy

If you are having a day where something is askew with your appearance (you ran out of shampoo, sprouted a third eye on your forehead, or spilled wine on your blouse), do something special to *her* appearance to draw the attention away from your blemish. Adorn her in or decorate her with something that really takes the cake. If you just dribbled frosting on your shirt, for example, mash an even bigger piece of cake on her head. She will appreciate getting to lick off the frosting. If you break a heel, maybe dress her in her own heels. Don't worry about making her look foolish. Her self-esteem is nearly invincible. Remember that she's prone to farting loudly in public and likes to eat off the floor. She is hardly worried about what other people think.

The Perfect Match

Wearing clothes and accessories to match your little bitch is the best compliment you can give her. Just as you reveled in buying matching shirts and lipsticks with your school friends, she'll love marketing the special bond of your friendship for all the world to see.

There are so many ways you can accessorize and dress as a duo. Anything you wear she can wear, too. For example, you can turn one of your Chanel earrings into a necklace charm for her. Here are some other items you can shop for in pairs:

- Necklaces (a matching bracelet should fit her neck)
- Scarves, both silk and knit
- Barrettes and ponytail holders
- Hats and visors
- T-shirts
- Silk flowers for your hair and her collar
- Leg warmers and wrist cuffs

She Likes to Get Naked

A true naturalist, she favors her birthday suit over any accessory. Because she has fully embraced her inner HMB, she loves the feeling of freedom. Whether she is full-figured or slim, she is a confident supermodel at heart, and she loves accessories that show off her body. If you are not willing to move into a community of naturalists, you can respect her style by adorning her with unobtrusive jewels, lightweight collars, and other accoutrements she won't realize she is wearing. If it is chilly outside, wrap her in a stylish blanket. If it's warm and sunny, sprinkle her with body glitter and take her on a naked jog—or maybe even enter her in an upcoming bear-buns fun run. You might find you like it as much as she does.

CHAPTER 6

The Doggy Dominatricks

Ruff love

As her mistress, you must remember that some girls *like* to be punished. To exert the proper influence over your little bitch, you will want to invest in a vinyl cat suit for you and a black vinyl leash and studded collar for her. With the proper costuming, she will begin to understand that as your "little miss," your word is law.

Bad Girls Like to Be Disciplined

Maybe you have been spending too many late nights working on that project at the office or on that six-foot-two blonde whose teeth sparkle when he smiles. Either way, you find yourself surprised to learn your little bitch has not only chewed a hole in your sofa, but also shredded your favorite panties and eaten one of the shoes you special ordered for your best friend's wedding tomorrow. Naturally you're angry. In fact, she probably has never seen you so angry. You yell at her, telling her she is the worst roommate you've ever had and you can't understand why she is such a bad girl. Soon, though, you start to feel sorry for her. You think back to the first time you wrecked your parents' car. They were so angry, they grounded you for two months. You felt like you had really let them down. You told yourself that when you become a parent you would never be so mean. And now look at you.

A wave of sadness and guilt rushes over you. After all, you *have* been focusing on yourself lately, and the possessions she destroyed are *just* material things. You give your bitch a kiss, grab her leash, and race her to the car. Driving with the top down, you head out for ice cream. You watch her lick an entire scoop as it drips on your leather seats, and you laugh as she gobbles the cone. Then you spend the afternoon playing in the park.

Six months later, however, you'll wonder why you have one pair of shoes left. (You are not dumb enough to leave the last pair on the floor.) Plus, you have one pillow left on your bed, you have to sleep in the fetal position so you won't roll into the hole she has chewed in your mattress, and your collection of favorite days-of-the-week panties now consists of "Monday" and "Wednesday"—your two least favorite days of the week. You can't understand why she is doing this to you. Every time you make up after a fight, she acts like she's going to be a good girl again.

The problem is that you've been rewarding her for being bad. And because she's home alone all the time, she is starved for your attention. The antidote is to spend quality time together. Teach her some tricks, and reward her for being good. When you run out of tricks, teach her to obey commands in French and Italian. Take her toy shopping and buy her a chewy purse and squeaky lipstick to play with. Find a guy who welcomes her on your dates, and take her to the office when you have to work at night. At the very least, hire a dog walker or drop her off at doggy daycare a couple days a week. If she behaves badly, do not confuse her. Let her know her actions are not OK. Pick up what's left of your "hursda" panties, lower your voice, show them to her, and say "no." Throw them in the trash and give her a fifteen-minute time out.

Discipline Through Rewards

Praise her. Tell her she is the greatest of all little misses. Buy a feather duster and tickle her nose to let her know when she's been a good girl. Also, keep a tube of your brightest red lipstick on hand. When she's good, kiss her in public. The more girls and bitches you see, the better. She will proudly wear your kiss like a gold star.

On her list of most important things, food ranks at the top—probably even more so than her love for you. Find a treat she likes and reward her in pea-sized servings. Just don't overdo it on the cookies: Once she's properly socialized, she will need to fit into that cute little black dress of hers.

Discipline Through Punishment

If you need to get her attention, use the end of the black vinyl leash you bought for her training. Whip it against a countertop or another hard surface to create a slapping sound. Never hit your little miss with it—just use it to get her attention and let her know you are in charge.

A few other suggestions for disciplining your bad little bitch include the following:

"Hose" her down with a spray bottle. Believe it or not, the punishment she will fear most is a spray bottle. You can buy one at any drugstore. Fill it with water. She will hate being sprayed and likely will remember the first time you spray her when she's bad. The next time she is bad, just pick up the spray bottle and shake it. If she knows what's good for her, she will stop misbehaving immediately.

Ignore her. If she is doing something bad, do not reward her naughty act with your attention unless she is putting her life, or your favorite stilettos, in danger.

Lock her up and throw away the debris. If she chews something up or creates a mess, put her in her crate. Do not let her see you cleaning up after her. Allow her to spend a few minutes considering your disappointment in her. Wait at least 15 minutes, then kiss and make up.

Note: *At first you will want to dominate her in privacy, away from distractions. Later you can test her devotion by dominating her in the presence of distraction.*

Trust

Trust will be an important factor in the dominatrix-miss relationship. If she can trust you, she easily will come to worship at your feet. It is OK to compromise her inner HMB—in other words, to get her to submit to your will—for her own safety. Always show her love and kindness. She is your number-one priority: You feed her, clothe her, give her a safe place to live, and pay her credit card bills. She wants to behave for you. It's up to you to show her how.

Note: *For decades, people have compared training dogs to training men. Now you know it is much easier to train dogs.*

She Does Tricks, She Loves Treats

Your little miss must be on her best ladylike behavior if she wants to accompany you in most social settings. If she is planning to travel with you, tag along on a shopping spree, or simply ride in the shopping cart at the grocery store, she will need to know these basics.

Cookie Hypnosis

One of the best ways to get your little bitch to do anything you want—sit, curtsy, wink at a cute guy across the bar—is to bribe her with a cookie. To do this, take the treat and run it through your fingers. Watch as your little bitch becomes immediately mesmerized. Tell her, "Keep your eye on the cookie . . . you're getting very tired . . . my wish is your command . . ."

Once she's hypnotized, repeat, "Sit, sit, sit . . ." while dangling the cookie above her nose and gently pushing her hiney toward the floor. You can use cookie hypnosis to teach her any other trick your heart desires. Make sure you have enough cookies on hand in case she doesn't get it right the first time: A pile the size of the carton of ice cream you ate the last time you got dumped should do nicely. Soon, every time she hears the magic word—whether it's "sit," "shake," or "flirt"—she will obey. You'll have her eating out of the palm of your hand (literally) in no time.

Stay

Once your little bitch is an ace at pushing her cushion to the floor (sitting), you can teach her to stay. First get her to sit. Next, put your hand up in front of you like you're one of Diana Ross's Supremes motioning for her to "stop in the name of love." Then take a step backward and tell her to "stay." If she obeys you, give her a cookie and the kind of big kiss that leaves lipstick on her forehead. If she gets up to walk toward you, start over from the sitting position. Have her practice "stay" repeatedly. Each time you do, take two steps backward—kind of like when you got back together with your ex-boyfriend—so that she's having to stay put from a farther and farther distance. She will eventually get it, and hopefully so will you. The trick is to keep treating her with love and cookies.

Fetch

She's probably a natural at this. Most girls enjoy the chase. And her loyalty will always bring her back to you. To teach her to fetch, gently toss one of her toys a few feet away from you and tell her to "fetch." When your lady returns with the toy, praise her. If she catches the toy in midair, praise lavishly, kissing her on the head when she returns. Also reward her with one of her favorite cookies. Do this repeatedly until you're sure she's gotten the hang of it. Don't worry: The exercise will keep her in shape. Supermodels eat cookies, too.

Come

This trick is fun to practice: You will need a very long leash or rope for it. Twenty feet will do. While holding the leash handle, command your little bitch to sit and then stay. Then take ten big steps away from her. Now say "come" and show her a cookie while gently pulling on her leash and directing her toward you with great enthusiasm. When she arrives in front of you, tell her how much you love her and give her the cookie. You must make this fun so that she wants to do it. Practice this command repeatedly. It may be the most important one she will learn. Always look happy when you command her to come, especially if she is in danger. If she senses anger or disapproval, she might be tempted to disobey you. Reward her with kisses and cookies and she'll pick it up that much faster.

Your Girl Likes to Potty All the Time

A couple weeks after she has made herself comfortable in her new home (yours), you probably will realize your little bitch potties like a rock star. If your home were a hotel, you surely would have lost your damage deposit by now, as your house is beginning to smell like the public restroom in the park.

Can you imagine your embarrassment if you met a cute guy at the grocery store and after eyeing you with interest, he caught wind of the air freshener, carpet cleaner, and urine-stain remover in your shopping cart? He'd look at you again, notice your four-legged wonder riding sidesaddle in your cart, and practically pinch his nose. The secret would be out: Your little bitch can't learn the basics, your house smells like pee, and the two of you are dirty girls.

The first step in potty training her is to glamorize pee. Call it something else, like "lemon drops" or "twinkle twinkle." Make sure to take her out first thing in the morning, just before she goes to bed, and ten minutes after each time she eats. Avoid feeding her a midnight snack, as she might have to make lemon drops after you've fallen asleep. If she is having trouble telling you she has to "go" at night, get her some puppy pads—absorbent diaperlike marvels that will save your carpet every time. Put down some pads in the bathroom so she will become familiar with them. She can even use them as her personal toilet if she has an emergency. If you cannot remove the smell from your house after she is potty trained, consider moving to a new place.

She Lets Her Body Do the Talking

Without saying a word, she communicates her excitement, disappointment, and anger, as well as many other emotions. She is an HMB through and through and will rely on you to figure out for yourself what she's thinking.

> *It wasn't the stars, it wasn't the moon.*
> *She simply studied her body from across the room.*
> *Doggy psychics aren't worth the cost.*
> *Crystal balls were meant to be tossed.*

She's All Stressed Out

If she has her tail tucked between her legs and won't look you in the eye, she's probably upset about something. Most likely, she feels a bit like you do when you've had a bad day at work. Remember, Girl's Best Friend is very sensitive to your own feelings and dramas. Your bad day could stress her out, too. Should you observe this behavior in her, make a 911 pedicure appointment for the two of you right away. You can also help her work off the day's stress by giving her a squeaky-free chew toy.

She Wants to Play

Her ears are back, her tail is flirtatiously wagging, and she's lunging forward with her hiney in the air. She's inviting you to play, an invitation you should accept as often as possible.

She's Easy

Rolling over on her back says she's easygoing. She's letting you know that she's a good girl, she wants to please you, and she doesn't plan to hurt you. Just be nice to her and call her in the morning.

A Lesson in Aggression

She's showing her teeth, leaning forward on her toes, pricking up her ears, and wrinkling her nose. It can only mean one thing: She's feeling protective and maybe even a little pissed off. For example, when the two of you are in your favorite department store to return that blouse you changed your mind about and the girl behind the counter gives you some trouble, you may sense a little hostility in your favorite companion. Distract your little bitch by pulling out her favorite squeaky lipstick. Be sure to let the salesperson know that you just saved her life.

She's a Bad Girl

Here are eight of the most predictable things she will do to wreak havoc:

1. Victoria's secret snack. **The little bitch destroyed your panties.**
The solution: Don't leave your panties on the floor.

2. Paws and relax. **She jumped up on you, leaving muddy paws on your sexy new dress.**
The solution: Drop her off at the pet sitter before you dress for the party.

3. She's a whiner. **No explanation needed—that's just high maintenance.**
The solution: Give her more attention.

4. Possessive bitch. **She's incessantly barking, yapping, growling, biting others to protect you, and tormenting the cat.**
The solution: Figure out if your bitch is barking for a reason. Sit down for a diva-to-dog therapy session, trying to get to her motivations. If she's barking out the window, look out with her and see what distresses her. Explore her problems with the cat, the mailman, or your gorgeous neighbor. She may be afraid of losing you, or she just may be lacking attention, and this is her method of disciplining you.

5. Destructive bitch. She's behaving like a very bad rock star and trashing your house.

The solution: This little bitch has issues. Maybe she is spending too much time alone. Do some training with her. She will relish your attention. She can only eat what she can reach.

6. Little thief. She's stealing and hoarding your stuff.

The solution: She is exhibiting insecurities. Hoarding your receipts, movie stubs, and old socks makes her feel safe when you are not there. She is putting together a stash of memories much like that box of memorabilia from your high school sweetheart. She doesn't think she's stealing; she thinks your things are hers for the taking. Let her hoard the insignificant stuff that won't hurt her and embrace her need to be with you.

7. The unexpected guest. The little bitch brought in a dead animal.

The solution: Remind her that real fur is socially unacceptable. Buy her a faux fur coat and supplement her diet with more protein.

8. Trashy behavior. She's forever raiding the garbage can.

The solution: Determine whether she's hungry or just curious. Her desire to raid the trash is a lot like yours to read gossip columns: She doesn't know why it's so intriguing. Keep the trash hidden away so she cannot explore it.

When to Hire a Professional Dom

Maybe you are too busy to dedicate time to your little bitch's training. Or maybe you want your relationship with her to be 100 percent fun. Or perhaps your little miss doesn't want to obey. Maybe she wants to be so much like you that she cannot fully submit to the idea of your controlling her. She fails to see the fun in the discipline. Instead, she thinks you're easy and knows she can get away with murder. Kind of like when you were growing up: Mom was the easy one, while Dad was the disciplinarian.

This is where a professional dominatrix can help. She is unattached to your little bitch. Training dogs is her life's work. She lives for discipline, and she won't cave like you do when your little bitch bats her eyes. To find a referral for a professional dom, look in the phone book, ask your friends, even ask your little bitch's friends. Whether you sign up for a private session or a group session (in other words, dog school), be sure to tell your dom what you want your bad little bitch to learn.

Note: *If your dom is unable to tame your dog, she will probably fire you before you fire her. She'll probably do this by excusing her inability to dominate your dog with a cavalier comment like, "Your dog's too smart," "She has so much confidence," or "She thinks for herself." This may very well be the case. After all, your pup is a stubborn HMB. And we all know it's no fun for a dom who's not in charge.*

CHAPTER 7

High Maintenance Etiquette

Life with her will be full of her little surprises

There's a good chance your little bitch really was born in a barn, and when it comes to teaching her manners, she will probably do a lot worse than just leaving the door open.

Whether it's making unwanted advances toward your guests when they arrive at your door or pooping on a crowded street, you will want to be prepared for any situation where she's left you *holding the bag.*

Puppy PDA

Because she loves you, she will want to give you a little lick every now and then just to show you how much she cares. Of course, you don't mind if she wants to steal a quick smooch periodically. After all, you kiss the top of her head forty-nine times a day, like a good mommy should. But every so often she will pick the most inappropriate time to show you her affection.

Take last month, when you were stuck in that traffic jam and your favorite new song was playing on the radio. Just as you were cranking up the volume, you noticed the hot guy in the sports car next to you smiling at you, adjusting his dial. You smiled back, slightly embarrassed but mostly tingling. Then suddenly, there she was—straddling your lap, her butt against the steering wheel. As if in slow motion, her little head lunged forward in a Tyrannosaurus Rex maneuver. Using only her open mouth, she went for the kill, leaving her useless forearms limp. Your eyes got huge, you tried to turn away, but your mouth didn't make it out of the way in time. So the sports car hottie had a front-row seat to the spectacle of you and your little bitch making out. You're pretty sure you'll never forget his expression of disbelief as he mouthed "Yuck!" and looked away. After that, you got wise and got her a car seat you could strap her into.

Mind Her Manners

Be certain that she will have her own bag of tricks, many of which will shock, surprise, or even upset you. But remember that the two of you are best friends—unconditionally, through thick and thin.

She Lets One Rip in Front of Your Boyfriend

It will happen when you least expect it. Maybe the three of you will be snuggled up on the couch with a movie on. Just you, Mr. Right, and Little Miss Inconsiderate. The movie will be the sideshow to tonight's real feature presentation, though: Just when you and he have started to smooch, the stench will cut between the two of you like a knife. His nose will do the "I dream of Jeanie" wiggle as he pulls away from you. You'll glance down at Little Miss Gaseous to find her fast asleep on her back, with all fours sticking straight up in the air, oblivious to the hideous aroma emanating from her.

How could she do this to you? You fantasize about smashing her puggy bank over her head, or at least docking her allowance for two months. But then you realize that you must think fast if you want to turn this into a positive situation. As the stink becomes more apparent and you and your sweetheart look at each other with unbridled embarrassment, you consider your options. If you ignore the smell, he might think that you did it. If you blame it on her, he might still think that you did it. So it's clear that your only option is to blame it on him. He will be so worried that you really do think it was him that he will explain to you it must be her, that's the only logical explanation. He'll never even think to blame her horrendous faux paw on you. Of course, if you ever do accidentally poot, you can always blame it on her.

She Puts Her Nose in Other People's Business

Because she is a curious creature, it can be hard to keep her out of other people's business. But your friends won't appreciate the fact that she knows they are wearing their "Saturday" panties on Wednesday. Nor will they be thrilled that she can discern everywhere they have been in the last few days, what they did there, and who they talked to—all by sticking her head between their legs. But she is a four-legged detective by nature, blessed with an impeccable sense of smell, and when she picks up a scent, collecting all of this information is addictive to her. To her, a simple sniff sniff at a friend's drawers is as normal as a handshake is to you. Therefore, it will be hard to break her of this habit. (Can you imagine if you had to stop shaking hands for the rest of your life?) After all, she practically grew up in a nudist colony, and her friends usually show up naked. So not much is left to her imagination and nothing is sacred.

If she continues to smell your friends in areas they are not comfortable with, try spraying a few squirts of sour apple on the back of their pants or skirt when they aren't looking. Pick a spray that is clear so it won't stain, but choose one with a strong odor. Your little bitch will hate this smell, and after this happens time and time again, with friend after friend, she will begin to associate this strong, sour odor with her inappropriate sniffing and will eventually stop.

She Thinks Your House Is Her Mosh Pit

The last time you went to a concert, you stupidly wore those delicate little sandals you'd just blown an entire paycheck on. Bursting with excitement, you made your way to the front of the stage, where you waited for the band to come on. You couldn't believe you'd gotten up front. As the opening band took the stage and the music began blaring, the previously friendly, nonviolent crowd turned into a sea of zombies smashing into each other. The girl that had offered you a stick of gum earlier now elbowed you in the side of the face. "Move, bitch!" she said, as she pushed her way to the stage. In the sea of madness, you said goodbye to those sandals. When you finally made it back to your car, you were out of breath, barefoot, and numb on the whole left side of your head.

You'll have flashbacks of that fateful night if your little bitch starts to slam dance when guests come over. She may begin to jump uncontrollably and dive bomb your furniture and each new guest who comes through the door. The rising hair on her head may even begin to resemble a mohawk as she moves through the air. This is when you need to become the Event Security for your home. Teach her that your guests are the "talent" and that she is a "fan" who must abide by the club rules. If she tries to rush the stage one more time, tell her "You're outta here!" Then grab her by her spiked collar and throw her out on her ass, into the backyard.

She Humps Your Niece's Teddy Bear

At the last family function, she was scared by the children—so scared, in fact, that you were afraid she might bite one of the little moppets. This time you take control of the situation and offer to put her in your niece's room where you won't have to worry about her. Hours later, you head back to your niece's room to retrieve her, grinning to yourself as you replay the unforgettable moments you just had with the cute caterer after his shift ended: the soft music, the strong wine, the dimly lit room, the dirty dancing by the fire. You walk in on a similar scene when you open the door to find your little bitch riding your niece's new stuffed bear. Huck the thing in the trash and get the hell out of there.

She Humps a Stranger's Leg

Maybe it was the astonishment you felt when she humped the leg of your boss the first time you brought her in to work. Or maybe it was the way it made you blush when she started to hump the leg of that that new guy you liked. And what about all those times she humped the gardener, the paperboy, and the mailman? Enough is enough, you finally tell yourself. Something has to be done about her constant, indiscriminate humping. You've grown tired of having to explain her actions every time. So instead, you turn the tables.

You realize all of these people are seducing *her* with their pats on her head, caresses on her ears and scruff, and free treats each time they see her. And like the mother of a blossoming teenage girl, you must remind these overgrown frat boys that you don't approve of them seducing your little bitch. The next time she starts humping the mailman, try announcing loudly to him (and the rest of the neighborhood), "She's a little young for you, don't you think?"

She Played All Day and Now She's Pooped

If anyone can glamorize poo, you and your little bitch can. Remember, you were the first of your friends to embrace bell bottoms again. And you had a thing for orange before everyone else. You're a cosmopolitan girl through and through, and even cosmopolitan girls need to clean up after themselves—or their trophy woof—every now and then.

All the girls know you're a trendsetter, so if you say poop-scooping accoutrements are the next big thing, they will be. Here are some of the most stylish (and practical) of poop-retrieval accessories:

- A furry grip that Velcros around the handle of her leash and opens up into a faux fur pocket, where you can store her rose-scented pink poo bags

- Said rose-scented pink poo bags, which have funny sayings on them like, "Poo, she did it again"

- As an alternative, expensive plastic bags from high-end department stores like Chanel or Saks

- A glittery wristlet-sized tote that attaches to her leash with a string of pearls or rhinestones

- A separate Velcro sleeve that attaches to her collar for storing fresh bags

- A little bit of her favorite perfume spritz so you can spray her hiney after she goes

- Baby wipes or Handi Wipes

The Gospel of HMB

It's your duty as a fellow HMB owner to spread the word when you see a girl jogging with her bitch and her bitch's bag-o-waste is slung around her collar. Yell after this dog owner that she should throw the waste in a bush if she cannot find a trash can. Tying poop bundled in an old plastic grocery bag around her little bitch's neck is *tres* tacky.

Faking the Pickup

At your best friend's wedding you were the girl with the safety pins, sewing kit, and double-sided tape, ready for any wardrobe malfunction. But at some point in your busy life you will find yourself unprepared and possibly embarrassed when your little bitch makes an unexpected deposit. At this point these are your options:

- Own it. Stand proudly beside the pile, waiting for a Good Samaritan with an extra bag to come along. Remember that once you own it, escape may be difficult, even precarious.

- Leave it. But then you risk the chance of being outed by the community poop patrollers. If they catch you, it could be a very humiliating conversation.

- Better yet, simply fake it. Women have been doing this for years. Be resourceful. Pretend you're getting a bag out of your pocket and bend in such a way that you block the poop. Gently slide a couple leaves over the top of the pile. Or if grass is all you have available, with a mighty burst of strength, quickly rip the roots from the earth, cover the pile, and "leaf it" there. Remember, it's all in going through the motions. Beware of any approaching meddlers—a passerby with a keen sense of smell could blow your cover. Then walk briskly in the other direction. It is important to immediately abandon the evidence.

Her Favorite Pickup Line

Only a few HMBs will experience the ultimate form of chivalry, a rare and revered gesture that's one of the greatest unspoken pickup lines in the history of flirtation. Here's what it looks like:

You and your doggy diva are playing at the park to work off the carbs after a tasty lunch at your favorite outdoor café. As she frolics in the grass, you become preoccupied by a Hollywood handsome in gargantuan sunglasses. Part of the fun of making eyes at him is your obvious attraction to your own reflection in his big eye mirrors. Thinking your grin is all for him, he advances toward you. And that's when your little bitch races around the corner and comes to a dead stop. She plants all four feet in the grass, squats down, tilts her head over her shoulder, and gives you a wink. In the midst of the pure-sexual-chemistry stare he's sharing with you, Hollywood sees it too—the soft-serve smoothie your bitch has prepared just for you. She smiles and runs away, and there it sits like a Hershey's kiss.

You take a moment to envision the horror of him watching you pick up her poop. You hear the sound of his car keys jingling in his pocket, and you realize it's all over. But then you hear another sound, the rustle of plastic. A true gentleman—no, a prince—he whips out a bag, steps past you, bends down, and picks up her pile.

Never let a man like this get away.

CHAPTER 8

Bitch About Town

She walks barefoot in the city

Every time you ask her what she's in the mood to do, her answer will be "I don't care, what do you want to do?" She knows you pilot her social scene and she is happy to fly shotgun everywhere you go. She will never tire of shopping. And at lunch or dinner you'll never have to request a doggy bag for her— you will find her ordering off the menu for the two of you. As you brave the risk of sneaking her in to more NDAs, the two of you will relish in shared adventure.

Dog-fensive Driving

Inevitably you and she will go for a ride in the car together. She will be panting beside you in the passenger seat, looking at you adoringly, her boa blowing in the wind. As you glance in your mirror at a red light to apply that sexy shimmer to your pouty lips, a car smashes into yours from behind. Even a tiny fender bender like this could lead to the death of your most treasured friend: If the passenger-side air bag inflates, it could tragically kill your little bitch on impact. The warning label on the visor that has the little red circle with the line through it says, "No baby, no kids." It doesn't say, "No dogs," but it should.

You can easily avoid this nightmare. If she is the size of an infant or a toddler, she should never ride shotgun. Itsy-bitsy bitches should ride in the backseat. (Tell her that you're her chauffer, and she gets to sit in the back, celebrity style.) Have a special elevated seat created just for her. That way she can see out the window and bark at passing studs hanging their tongues out of sports cars. If she's a big bitch and wants to copilot in the front seat, you should at least harness her and buckle her in.

She's So Hot

On warm days, don't leave her in the car. Not even for two minutes. No exceptions. Always keep a bottle of Evian on hand for her. If she's hot after traveling in the car with you, have a pet T-shirt contest and pour the bottle on her to cool down. Tell her first prize is not overheating.

In-dog-nito (How to Sneak Her in Almost Anywhere)

Remember when your sorority sister turned twenty-one and she scored you a fake ID so you could go out clubbing with her? You drank your first dozen martinis; met a slew of sophisticated, older men; and stayed out dancing till dawn at some of the most glamorous clubs in town. Those were the days. You will always be grateful your sorority sister included you. Your little bitch will feel this same gratitude if you sneak her into your favorite hotspots. She'll feel as though she's just joined the secret HMB sorority of Alpha Alpha Alpha.

When you're sneaking her into an NDA establishment, often a sexy smile will be enough to distract the bouncer, security guard, or maître d'. But in some stuffier bars, department stores, and restaurants, it will take more than a little innocent flirting and a boob job to get your bitch in the door. You'll need a little ingenuity and a lot of sass. Here is our almost-foolproof method:

Dress her up as a service dog and prepare to be served. Service dogs—which assist people with conditions such as seizures, blindness, hearing impairment, depression, and anxiety—are often permitted where other dogs are not. Never let anyone pet your service dog while she's "working." She will love the attention and won't be able to play the part of the well-mannered, stoic bitch. A working service dog does not wag her tail, wiggle her butt, and whine to be petted.

In addition to dressing her as a service dog, here are some other tips:

🐾 Smuggle her in. Try to sneak her past all bouncers, security guards, and maître d's. Use your purse, a maternity shirt, a blanket, or anything else you can think of.

🐾 Shut her up at all costs. If she's about to bark, point your finger at her nose adamantly to let her know who's the alpha bitch. You might also remind her of the days when taking her shopping meant leaving the car window cracked open.

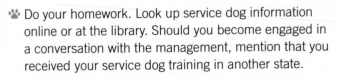

❧ Do your homework. Look up service dog information online or at the library. Should you become engaged in a conversation with the management, mention that you received your service dog training in another state.

❧ "I left my wallet in the car." If you are asked to provide paperwork proving she is a working girl, this is your only answer. When you get to the car, drive away at top speed.

In most cases, the two of you will soon be drinking lattes or martinis, shopping for shoes, and watching your favorite movies on the big screen. You could be a pioneer in a new canine-rights movement. Think about it: Women weren't allowed to apply for their own credit cards until the 1970s. Maybe the tides are finally turning for their canine counterparts.

Note: *When sneaking her into places, avoid all real service dogs and all moppets. They will blow your cover.*

Approach Moppets with Caution

Moppets (a.k.a. children under the age of ten) can be small, fast, and unpredictable. When you and your little bitch are out on the town, you're likely to encounter what may seem like an army of them along the way. Moppets often will express an urgent desire to commune with your bitch, and their representatives (a.k.a. guardians) will ask you to indulge them. To try to persuade you, a moppet representative may flash you a friendly smile and call your four-legged diva a "cute little doggy." Do not succumb to such solicitations. Your little bitch is not from a petting zoo. She has mood swings like anyone else. If repeatedly rushed by moppets, she may start to wonder, "Why do strangers always think they can put their filthy paws all over me?"

If forced to interact with moppets against her will, your bitch's reaction may mirror that of the college roommate whose food you always ate and phone you always tied up with six-hour calls to your long-distance boyfriend. After months of telling you, "No problem—go ahead," one day the sky turned black, thunderclaps shook the room, and Ms. It's All Good let you have it. All her pent-up resentment tore through the surface like a rupturing volcano, and she ripped your head off. Likewise, your little bitch may oblige her moppet suitors for months, even years, then suddenly decide she can't take their incessant poking and fur pulling anymore. Pushed to her limit, she may growl or bark ferociously; she may even attempt to bite off a moppet's nose.

Needless to say, this could have some extremely serious consequences: The city could imprison your precious princess, the moppet representative could take you to court (and to the cleaners), and the powers that be could even sentence your bitch to death. To avoid such altercations, tell any moppet representative who requests the attention of your bitch that she is busy shopping. If the moppet starts to whine in protest, ask the representative if the moppet is friendly and if you can pet him or her. Chances are, if you turn the tables, they'll scurry off in no time.

Dude, Where's My Dog?

It happens at least once in every child's life. Maybe it was when you were six. You and Mom were doing a little Saturday shopping. As she slowly pushed the cart from rack to rack, you took your small body and ducked inside the rack, between the clothes, and peeked out, trying to see when she would find you. Twenty minutes later, you had already emerged from the rack, but as you wandered the aisles, it became painfully clear you had lost Mom. As you started to cry, the saleslady took you to the front of the store, asked your name, called for your parent on the loudspeaker, and waited for someone to come claim you. Your mother soon approached looking worried and shaken, like she had been frantically looking for you, too.

Fast forward a couple of decades: You are worried and shaken. You think, "Oh, NOOOOO! Where could I have left her?" You frantically rack your brain, trying to remember the last time you had her. Wasn't she in her carry bag in the dressing room when you tried on that cute little black skirt? You're pretty sure she was sitting on the cosmetic counter when you tried on that lipstick, and she was definitely at your side, cheering you on, when you bought that pair of $300 heels. As you dig through your shopping bag, hoping to find some sort of clue, that is when you find her, fast asleep at the bottom of the bag.

In case she isn't in your shopping bag, here are some tips for finding her:

1. Check your receipts to see where you have been. Check each of those stores.

2. Check all of her favorite stores to make sure she isn't just doing a little shopping on her own.

3. Have her paged on the loudspeaker in each store. Make sure the employee announces that she has a flesh-eating virus. This will deter anyone from stealing her or accidentally taking her home.

She's Outta Sight

The only thing more frightening than breaking two freshly manicured nails at once is thinking you may have lost her forever. To prevent this from happening, make sure she always wears her nametag, complete with your current cell phone number and e-mail address, on her collar. You may even want to invest in a GPS tracking device for her in case she gets lost. You also can attach a Velcro pocket to her collar and put twenty bucks inside so whoever finds her can put her in a cab and send her home to you. (In addition, if you run out of cash, you can borrow it from her.)

If you do lose her, here's how you can act fast to get her back:

- Blanket the area with a "missing" flyer that includes a picture of her, the date she was lost, and your contact info. Put flyers on every telephone pole within a 3-mile radius. Tell all your neighbors and local businesses to keep an eye out for her.

- Call a pet locator service that uses dogs who track the scent of missing pets. They will use her favorite blanket, boa, or anything else with her scent on it to sniff her out. You can also go online at www.globalpetfinder.com.

- Call your local TV news show and invite them to watch the locator-dog hunt for her. Tell the reporter that your little bitch is (1) famous for saving your family from a fire back when you lived in Idaho, (2) a family member's service dog, or (3) the star of dozens of European TV commercials. Desperate times require desperate measures.

Whining and Dining

Although shopping together at the grocery store can be fun, you'll both want to dine out more often than not. As neither one of you likes doing the dishes at home, you'll be eager to experience the restaurant world and all of its cuisine together. Once you have mastered slipping into NDA establishments, you can enjoy the rewards of dining at your favorite restaurants with your little bitch in tow. She's sure to enjoy these dishes:

Italian

When eating at a romantic Italian restaurant, order her pasta with a little parmesan sprinkled on top. Or get her the mini pizza with cheese and Canadian bacon.

Japanese

No sushi for her; it's not worth chancing her getting sick if the raw fish is old. She will enjoy a California roll with cooked salmon instead.

Mexican

She'll have the quesadilla with chicken and light cheese on a corn tortilla.

Chinese

Her favorites are pot stickers or chicken and rice. Be sure to get her a fortune cookie, too.

Burgers

Order her a meat patty or an unbreaded chicken breast. She will love this burger more than the many yappy meals you have gotten her in the drive-thru.

Dessert

She loves ice cream and crème brûlée best. Always share dessert with her, as long as it's not chocolate.

Note: *If you notice a dog chained up outside a restaurant waiting for her owner, assure your girl you would never leave her out there like that, a potential victim to moppets and abduction. Tell her she is a precious diamond. The same people who tied up their little bitch like that probably locked their car, yet they leave her there all alone and defenseless.*

Nickname Her after a Celebrity

One of the best ways to deal with an NDA restaurant is to nickname your dog after a celebrity. Choose a high-profile person who suits her and call her this name before the two of you go out to your favorite NDA establishment. For example: "Demi Moore, want to go out to dinner?" When she hears you call her by her celebrity nickname, she will know it is time to get dolled up for a fancy dinner.

Call ahead to make reservations and use her celebrity name ("I'd like to reserve a table for two at 8 p.m. The name is M-O-O-R-E. Demi Moore . . ."). When you arrive at the restaurant, tell the maître d' that you are her assistant. Then prepare to enjoy the best dinner ever. If this doesn't happen, or if the two of you are turned away because of the establishment's NDA policy, defend her like any good celebrity assistant would. Cause a scene, speaking in a voice loud enough for all the other patrons to hear: "Demi Moore is not happy! She cannot believe how you treated her! Demi Moore is never going to eat here again!" You may lose a little dignity on your way out, but the irreversible damage you cause the restaurant will well make up for it.

Note: *As they escort the two of you out, if you are still starving, see whether they will put together a little doggy bag for the two of you to share.*

Take Her to Work with You

With all the sneaking around you two have been doing, you will be sorely tempted to sneak her into your workplace. So why not try some of the same excuses for bringing her into the building at your job? If mere strangers are gullible enough to believe that she's a service dog or celebrity, the people who trust you surely will not suspect that you are stretching the truth. Tell your boss that she detects seizures and must accompany you at all times from now on. If your boss has any objections, let him know that she has experience in paper shredding.

Get to work early the first day you bring her and make coffee. Walk around the office and serve the coffee to them on a rolling cart. Have her sit on a little cushion on the top of the cart (but far enough from the coffee so freaky germ people don't complain) and tell everyone that she brewed it herself. They will know you are lying but will think that it is cute. Make her a permanent spot at your desk so people know that she is here to stay. Put a little "Assistant" sign above her.

If you want to butter up the boss, start working longer hours. Then tell him that since you've had her there the time just flies by. He will like her around if he thinks it will be easier to slave-drive you. Try teaching her how to fetch the faxes off the machine. (This may require lowering the machine to the floor. Be aware that this may cause some complainers to whine that they don't like to bend down or that they have back problems.)

If your colleagues are pleased with her work, start campaigning to get her on the payroll. There is no reason why she shouldn't be able to earn some money for herself. Then get her business cards and all the other employee accoutrements. It will be easier for people to treat her like a colleague when they see she has her own e-mail address and phone extension.

Every Dog Has Her Date

It's a dog eat dog world when it comes to finding friends for your little girl. Here are some ways you can ensure that her dance card is always full:

Her Newsletter

Superimpose photos of her with those of celebrities and public dignitaries on the pages of her monthly newsletter. Her friends will certainly be impressed when they see she was at John Travolta's Dogs Disco and Adam Sandler's Bitches Bark Mitzvah. And when they see she's rubbing elbows with Jennifer Lopez and having slumber parties with Paris Hilton's Tinkerbell, they will all want to rub noses with her. Get your bitch her own address book or BlackBerry so she can keep track of her newsletter mailing list. She should be willing to contribute a portion of her allowance for postage.

The Bitch Needs Some Swag

Every mover and shaker needs a social card, and she's no exception. On your computer, design some cards she can pass out to new friends in the mall or at the pooch park. Remember, you are marketing her so she can have the most friends and get invited to the best parties.

Her card might include the top reasons she is fun to play with:

🐾 She loves wrestling in the mud.

🐾 She rolls on her back when dominated.

🐾 She shares her treats.

🐾 She's into both group play and one-on-one.

Feel free to use her picture on her card, too. Use Photoshop to give her picture an exotic background or to place her at the bar with a martini in front of her. Make sure her cell phone number is on the card, too.

Get That Bitch a Web Site

Offer to post upcoming parties for your canine community. She is guaranteed to get invited to them all. Document her social comings and goings on this site, and be sure to include pictures of her at all the parties she attends. If you brand her as a party girl, her friends will begin to believe she is truly the life of every party. Some additional tricks include these:

🐾 Use her showgrowl name (see page 12).

🐾 Offer to post pictures and profiles of her friends.

🐾 Post her fashion tips, shopping suggestions, restaurant reviews, and bristling quotes.

🐾 Promote her escort services with the text, "Is your dog looking for some bitch companionship?" Include her cell phone number.

Note: *Do not be afraid to blacklist any dogs that do not invite her to their parties. For instance, if Spot turns six and invites everyone but her to his birthday gala, you could make this post to her site:*

PUBLIC HEALTH ANNOUNCEMENT: *Those who attended Spot's sixth birthday party should see a veterinarian, due to a ringworm breakout among several guests.*

CHAPTER 9

Dating, Mating, and Salivating

*There's no such thing as a third wheel
on the road to love*

When "search for a mate" means more than rummaging around for that other shoe under the bed, your little bitch will play a key role in helping you choose a potential beau or simply helping you score a date with him Friday night. With the two of you working together, there will be no limits to who you will meet, how you will reel him in, and what the two of you will do with him once you get him.

"Should We Get a Boyfriend?"

Asking your boyfriend, "Honey, should we get a dog?" is so passé. Any self-respecting girl knows that her little bitch is always first and foremost in her life. But when the urge arises to adopt a member of the hairier sex, by all means consult your little four-legged love. She can help you choose a good male by asking the right questions.

How Old?

Although the idea of a young stud may have a certain appeal, training an energetic youth can require an extraordinary amount of time and patience. Sure, watching your adopted male learn new tricks and grow into his skin may be fun. But young pups can be squirmy, spastic, and easily distracted. And all this can translate into added stress and lost beauty sleep for you. On the other hand, the size, temperament, and activity level of a mature male will be obvious from the get-go. Plus, adult males usually are housebroken and know the basic commands.

What's His Background?

Ask these questions to learn more about him:

1. Are you a "turn in" (divorced) or a stray (never been married)?

2. If you were turned in, why did your previous owner give you up? (Any insights into his past can be helpful in training him.)

3. Do you have any behavioral issues I should know about? More specifically, are you potty trained? Aggressive? Prone to chewing women's underwear?

4. Are you hyperactive? How much daily exercise do you require?

5. Have received all your shots?

6. Have you been altered?

How's His Temperament?

These effective tests can provide much of the information you need to determine whether he's a suitable fit for your home:

Sociability

Call your potential adoptee over to say hello. If he's friendly, he'll wag his tail and approach you with a grin that says he's eager for your attention. Be sure to introduce him to your little bitch. If he is good with dogs, he'll nuzzle right up to her and maybe even lick her snout.

Tolerance of physical affection

Determine how much contact he will tolerate by touching him about a dozen times during the course of several minutes. See how he reacts to being scratched behind the ears, pat on the head, and pet on the scruff of his neck. Notice whether he leans in or pulls away.

Excitability level

Invite your little bitch to a rowdy game of fetch. Run around and make noise until she's visibly excited. Pay attention to your potential new male's reaction. If he tells you to keep it down, he may be a bit too high maintenance—even for you. If he becomes aggressive with your little girl, he again may not be the best male for you. But if he becomes playful, enjoys the game, and can calm down quickly once it's over, he could be an excellent choice.

Response to new situations

Observe how your potential adoptee reacts in various settings. When you take him for a short walk, does he tend to sniff up others' skirts? Does he need practice, training, or even medication to remain calm in social situations? Males like this need obedience training, a good collar (perhaps a shock collar), and a short leash. In short, they may be more trouble than they're worth.

Note: *It is perfectly acceptable to drop your stud off at a shelter or simply give him away if he doesn't make an effort to respect you and your little bitch and behave in your home.*

Use Her as Your Wing Dog

Dog-friendly establishments make the best places for you and your bitch to sniff out a new male. Here are some tried-and-trues:

Home Depot

Does she imagine being held in the tan, strong arms of a carpenter or land developer? Or dream of marking her territory in the well-groomed yard of a sexy homeowner? Then it's time to hit the nearest home repair store, where the two of you can replace your light bulbs and get a date for Friday night all in one shot.

Before you go, remember to change your outfit. You may be working on your house, but you don't want all those home-improvement hotties to see you in sweats and a paint-spattered T-shirt, do you? Put on something clean, clingy, a tad revealing; add a little heel and some fresh makeup. Brush your teeth. Dress your four-legged accessory in something silly like a feather boa and a construction helmet, maybe with a sticker on the side that says "I'm a great cook." In the store, put her to work as a hood ornament on the front of your shopping cart.

When a worthy male asks if she really is a great cook, tell him you do all the cooking. Also tell him you think she likes him and if he's free Friday, you can prepare an Italian dinner for the three of you.

The Dump

She loves trash. It's dirty, it's intriguing, and it's filled with hidden treasures. (Besides, she knows you're apt to get a little trashy yourself every now and then.) So indulge her: Take her to the dump. If you've never been, you're about to find out that the dump is one of the best-kept secrets of single girls.

First, do your research; find a dumpsite that caters to an upper-middle-class demographic–based neighborhood. (If you set your eyes on too wealthy a neighborhood dumpsite, you're more likely to run into dump workers as opposed to home owners dropping off their own trash.) Then, offer to take all of the beer cans and champagne bottles from the party your best friend threw the night before. Also offer to get rid of that old dresser taking up space in her garage—you definitely need something you can't lift alone. Then have her help you fill your little brother's truck with these items. Dress your bitch with a tiara and diamond collar.

At the dump, stay in your parked car until a cutie pulls in. Then hop out and begin to remove the dresser. Slowly. Exaggerate how much you're struggling with it, telling your little bitch as you proceed that you wouldn't have to worry about moving such crap if the two of you had a boyfriend. Then flash him a sexy smile until he comes over to help. As the two of you unload the bottles and cans, tell him you have a lot of parties and maybe he can come to the next one.

The Fire Station

Everyone knows dogs look great next to fire hydrants and fire trucks. Which is precisely why you're going to pull out her best collar, dress her in a sexy red bikini, and visit your neighborhood fire station. Tell the firemen you're making a dog calendar for charity and ask if you can take some pictures of her posing on top of their shiny red truck.

While snapping photos, assess the age, background, and temperament of every stud in the room. Then ask the best-looking single fireman to join her in the picture. Perhaps he would even be willing to take his shirt off. As they pose together, tell him you may need to use his hose as you're taking some awfully hot photos. Once you have the pictures printed up, send him the best one. Include a note that says something like, "I think she really warmed up to you. Let's do this again." Be sure to include your phone number. Also try this tactic at police stations and military bases.

Dog Park Pickup Lines

As you watch your four-legged pride and joy prance from one end of the park to the other in her new tiara and diamond collar, you spot him: your dream man, over in the corner, adoringly throwing a slobber-covered toy at his own four-legged bundle of love. But how do you approach him? What do you say? Why not pretend you're a reporter doing a story on dog-park dating? Pull out a pen and little notepad, walk over, and ask if he'd mind answering these questions:

1. Are you single or married? (If he's married, tell him the story is on singles and find another guy to "interview.")

2. What would you do if a pretty girl caught your eye at the dog park?

3. Would the breed of her dog influence your interest in her?

4. How would you strike up a conversation with her?

5. How would you ask her out?

6. Where would you take her?

Now ask his *dog* these questions:

1. What is your average household income?

2. What kind of car does your human drive?

3. Is your master into toy breeds?

4. Does your owner date very often?

5. Does he ever take you his on dates?

6. What are your human's favorite hobbies?

7. Does your owner ever cook for you?

8. Would he ever sneak you into an NDA restaurant?

9. If you got another dog pregnant, how would your human handle the situation?

If you're still interested after he and his pooch have answered all your questions, tell him you don't normally mix business with pleasure, but you'd love to plan a playdate for your two dogs.

Love Bytes

It seems like a new Internet dating site for pet owners crops up every five minutes. As if cyberdating without dogs wasn't bad enough, now you have the opportunity to meet online thousands of losers *with* dogs. But it doesn't hurt to network: After all, many a loser met online will have a single brother or friend who's better looking and makes more money. If nothing else, Internet dating gives you and your little bitch an opportunity to meet average Joes who can introduce you to some real princes.

When creating an online dating profile for you and your bitch, you want to stand out from the pack so you attract men who are the pick of the litter. Co-opt all of your bitch's best traits for this, like her great hair, boundless energy, and long tongue. It is really no use competing with someone who has six nipples when marketing yourself to a population of panting males, so you may as well concentrate on *her* selling points. Men will most likely be interested in her hair color, height, weight, and interests, so you might create a profile that looks something like this:

Hair color: Dirty blonde
Height: 1 foot 2 inches tall
Weight: 12 pounds
Hobbies: Mud wrestling with playmates

Note: *It is important to only make dates with men who own small breeds. Large-breed dogs are not allowed to patronize the better restaurants. It's OK to make exceptions for the ultrahot guys you meet online because dining will be the last thing on your minds.*

Beauty and the Bees

In the waiting room of your veterinary clinic, you contemplate whether you're going to hell as the hives on her perfect little body swell into moguls—looking at them now, though, you envision you and her über-hot doctor skiing the slopes together and sipping cocoa at the chalet afterward. You awake from your reverie as the nurse calls her name.

You know you shouldn't have taken all that time to fix your hair, apply your lipstick, and change into a sexy dress before driving her over here, but can anyone blame you? The nurse guides you into an examination room, and you reassure your little bundle of joy that the doctor will be in shortly to save her life from that wretched bee sting, like a handsome hero in a summer blockbuster movie. When he walks in and asks what happened to her, it takes you a minute to remember. You're even having a hard time remembering her name, despite the fact that it's emblazoned in rhinestones on her collar.

You finally manage to tell him she was stung by a bee. Again. The vet laughs and jokes if you have a beehive inside your house because this must be her fourth sting this summer. Looking into his eyes, for a moment you consider the idea of adding a hive to your interior decor, but then you come to your senses. Instead, you tell the vet you think she is eating the bees because she has a crush on him. Funny thing is, *you* would be willing to eat bees to see him. It's then that you realize she is eating those stinging demons to help get you a date, that's how much she loves you. After the appointment, instead of asking the vet out, focus on your ailing little girl: Take her for some soothing gelato and tell her that you'll keep a spare lipstick and sexy blouse in the car for the next time.

Introducing Your Bitch to Your Stud

When you first introduce the two of them, you will have high hopes that they hit it off right away. You want him to adore her, and you especially want her to like him. Their first meeting is more about whether she likes him than vice versa, because if she does not like him, she will do everything in her power to sabotage your new relationship. She will constantly be peeing on his belongings or chewing up his shoes or just about anything she can think of to cause a conflict between you and him.

She is your best friend, which means she always gets jealous when you get a new boyfriend. It will only take one occasion to set her off, say if the three of you are laughing hysterically about the funny movie you saw last week, until she realizes that she never saw the movie because the two of you went without her. As she solemnly looks up at her fake service jacket (see page 91) hanging by the door (knowing full well you *could* have snuck her into the movie if you wanted her to go), she will tell herself that she will never forget this, and she will do everything in her power to get rid of him, even if it means running under the tire of his car.

Because her approval of him is so important, you should do whatever you can to help him win it. When he arrives at your house for the first time, step outside alone to greet him. Hurry to your car and fetch the bouquet of flowers and chewy bone you bought earlier. Tell him to give them to her as soon as he gets inside. She will run up to him with great excitement. She has heard so much about him and has looked forward to meeting him. The two of them will sniff each other a little and walk in circles around one another. Try not to get too involved. Let them work it out. If he gives her a cheesy compliment and acts nervous, it's a sign he likes her. If she leans against his leg for a pat on the head or a scratch on the belly, you know they are off to a good start—and you can breathe a sigh of relief.

Note: *The chewy will act as a great distraction if you haven't told her that you and he might be more than friends. She will be so busy chewing that it will take her longer to notice the two of you making out on the couch.*

Make Him a Dog Person

How's your new stud getting along with your bitch? Here's a "test" you can give him to find out.

Ask him, "Are you most happy when I'm happy?" Of course he'll say yes, but then turn the question around and tell him, "I'll only be happy if you love my dog." Then ask him, "Do you like the way I cook for you?" Then tell him, "I'll only cook for you if you love my dog." See how this works.

You can also test him with these questions:

- Do you like being seen with me in public?
- Do you enjoy touching my breasts?
- Do you like having sex with me?

In no time at all, you'll be able to sway him to love your bitch. That is, unless he runs off scared; he wasn't worth your time, anyway.

What If He's Allergic to Her?

Maybe it's the down feathers in your pillows? Or a peanut butter allergy? If your boyfriend is scratching and itching, and his eyes are watering, and he can't stop sneezing, there's a good chance he might be allergic to her. As his stare sweeps across the room like a pendulum, first directed at you, then at her, then back at you again, you need to act fast. You need to convince him it's not her that's making him sick. *You need to fake having a cat.*

If you've ever faked an orgasm, faking a cat will be a no-brainer. Act as though it doesn't occur to you that he might be allergic to your little bitch. After all, he has no proof. His red eyes could be running like faucets for any number of reasons. Tell him, "Oh, Honey Bunny, are you allergic to cats? My kitty, Mr. Bumbles, sheds everywhere." When he says, "You have a cat?" tell him of course you do, you've had Mr. Bumbles since you were twelve. But not to worry: Your sister (make up a sister, too, if you have to) just bought a house and it just so happens that she's taking in Mr. Bumbles in a week. For good. Also tell him that everyone *knows* people are more allergic to cats than dogs. Then explain that Mr. Bumbles, a big sexy tomcat, spends most of the day lying around in the neighbor's yard and most nights out chasing pussy, which is why he isn't here at the moment. Nothing like a sexual innuendo to make your teary, sniffling boyfriend forget that his head is swelling like a watermelon.

While he's still ruminating on the word "pussy," tell your honey, "Let's just avoid my place for the week, until Mr. Bumbles officially moves out." Then spend the next week putting this allergy-busting plan into action:

1. Hire a very hardworking housekeeper to come twice during the week to remove all your bitch's fur and dander.

2. Make your guy a drink and slip him a mickey (in this case, Benadryl). This is the only desperate measure that requires you to drug your man. Martinis are a great option for hiding an anti-allergy mickey. To make a High Maintenance Bitch martini, combine one shot of vodka with a glass of cherry cream soda and put some sugar on the rim. After your boyfriend downs the drink, tell him you're feeling frisky and start to pet him. If he associates his medicinal martini with good sex, he will never turn it down.

Note: *If he sees you slipping him the mickey, tell him it makes sex better. If he doesn't buy it, be honest: Tell him you didn't want to get rid of Mr. Bumbles because you've had him since you were twelve.*

She's Feeling Frisky, Too

You and your newly adopted sweetie get back from a nice, long candlelit dinner at your favorite restaurant. You've got a nice buzz from all that steak and cabernet, not to mention that intoxicating smooch he just planted on you in the driveway. You take your shoes off, he turns the stereo on. . . . There's only one thing that can stop this train to paradise: *her*.

Here are some of her favorite ways to kill the mood—and some ways you can prevent her from scaring off your boyfriend:

She Likes to Watch

You and your guy are riding on that proverbial freeway of love and bliss abounds. Suddenly you have that unsettling feeling that you're being watched. You look up and there she is, fixated on you, paralyzed with curiosity. You demand she leave the room. She sits immobile, a little over an arm's length away. If you could reach her, you would grab her by her diamond links and toss her out the door. You throw a pillow at her, hoping she will get the hint, but she offers up the bitchiest look she can muster. It's then you realize she likes to watch. For a moment you think you even see her smile.

When the party is over, have a talk with her. Tell her you understand she can relate to all that panting and begging, but there's no place for her in your little love nest. Next time, turn on Animal Planet for her in the living room and get her a bowl of pupcorn. If she scratches on the door, put a porno on for her instead. When you're finished being alone with your sweetie, the three of you can meet up and eat ice cream in bed together.

She Wants to Join In

Somewhere along the way all this talk about being a team player may have confused her. You may not actually realize she is participating in your bedroom antics until she's wrapped around your boyfriend's leg, or worse, putting her nose where it doesn't belong. Since you decided in college that you're not into threesomes, tell her this is mommy's time and she must go away. If she doesn't get the hint, you may have to put the "crate" in great sex.

Note: *Never use whipped cream while she's in the room. Getting rid of her will be a lost cause.*

She Thinks You're Being Attacked

You can only imagine how frightened she must have been when she heard you screaming. (She nearly called 911.) Startled out of her sleep, she awoke to witness you pinned underneath some life-threatening predator. She saw your contorted mouth and the strange, unfamiliar look on your face. You can't blame her for diving onto the bed to rescue you, growling, baring her teeth, and biting your man's thigh until he yelped in pain.

You realize it might take a while for her to understand the birds and the bees. Every time you lock her out of the bedroom, she cries and carries on, completely killing your romantic evening. "Stop!" you yell. "I'm fine. He's not hurting me." But, of course, there's no convincing her. So unless you want to have silent sex from now on, like some teenager doing it in her parents' house, schedule a couple of hours with her dog walker or puppy au pair so you and your date can be alone. Your boyfriend will be happy to cover the expense.

Note: *Try putting cotton in her ears to muffle the moans.*

Should You Make Him Sleep on the Floor?

Of course your new boyfriend will try to do everything to gain your attention. And although it is normal for him to be a little jealous of your relationship with your little bitch, beware of the man who is so territorial that he plans to move her out of your bed, or worse, out of your home altogether.

Signs he may be a frog in prince's clothing include making comments like these:

🐾 "Honey, there sure is a lot of fur in the bed."

Suggested response: "I never really noticed before. Could it be from your legs? Let's try shaving them and see if it's still a problem." Don't even entertain the notion that the fur could be coming from her.

🐾 "Wow, she sure can take up a lot of space for such a little thing."

Suggested response: "Imagine what she must be thinking of you. After all, she is sharing her side of the bed with you."

🐾 "Well, I slept alright, but she sure snores loudly for a pint-sized princess."

Suggested response: None. Do you really want such a princess for a man?

Watch out for other worrisome boyfriend behavior:

🐾 He refers to her as "the dog" rather than using her actual name.

Suggested response: "Rosalita has a name." Until he gets this straight, only talk about him in the third person and refer to him as "the boyfriend."

🐾 He has the arrogance to request that she sleep on the floor.

Suggested response: Tell him he ought to try it for a night. He obviously does not appreciate your love for her. This is a core value that cannot be compromised.

🐾 He directly asks her to sleep on the floor.

Suggested response: Decide right then and there whether you'll make him an outdoor boyfriend or simply dump him. Remember that when he's gone, she'll still be there to cuddle with you at night.

Always a Breedsmaid, Never a Bride

If you and your boyfriend decide to tie the knot, your bitch will of course want to partake in all the wedding festivities. She will roll in the discarded wrapping paper and bows at your bridal shower. She will pose for her picture with the stripper at your bachelorette party. And she will want the biggest slice of wedding cake on your big day.

When it's time to say your vows, your little bitch will want to be right by your side. After all, she watched your entire relationship blossom, and she remembers as fondly as you do that big bouquet of flowers and rawhide chewy your husband-to-be gave her on your first date. So it's only right you make her a bridesmaid. Imagine your groom waiting at the end of the aisle as she approaches in a satin gown and matching tiara of flowers on her head. She can be escorted by your maid of honor, your dad, or even you.

Her white wedding leash should be at least 20 feet long to allow for her show-stopping entrance, and it should be decorated with flowers. Her custom-fit gown should match those of the other bridesmaids. After you are pronounced husband and wife, the three of you should walk down the aisle together, you on his right arm, she on his left. Be sure to include her in at least one slow dance, preferably your first dance as husband and wife. And remember that when you and your new hubby cut the cake, you should smash some on her face, too (as long as it's not chocolate cake).

Note: *If she likes to watch, she should not be invited on the honeymoon.*

The Puppy Prenup

It may not work out with him, but her love is forever. In the event of a separation or divorce, you want to make sure he doesn't run off with your best friend. In the flushed moments of your wedding engagement, it may be hard to imagine yourself someday hating this man you love so much. And it may be even harder to imagine him cruelly, vindictively packing her along with his suitcase and taking her from your life forever.

If you do someday split from Mr. Wonderful, everyone knows how skilled she will be at consoling you as you cuddle and cry while she licks the tears and snot off your face in search of some remaining Ben & Jerry's ice cream. You need her by your side—till death do you part—as much as she needs you. Which is why you must retain custody of her should your marriage fizzle. It's your job to protect her from a life of licking empty peanut shells and spilled beer off the floor while your ex and his friends drool over the dancing girls in the half-time show.

To ensure you retain custody of her, you need to get her paperwork in order—*before you get married*. Have an attorney draw up a contract that states she is your property. And make sure the following are in your name only:

🐾 All her AKC papers

🐾 Her veterinary account

🐾 Her bill of sale or adoption papers

Note: *Only allow your ex visitation rights if your little girl agrees to it. If she does agree to the visits, charge him dog support to cover at least half of her expenses.*

CHAPTER 10

She's a First-Class Bitch

She taxis to the runway

When your little bitch told her friends of all the fun she had in the cabin, she had to laugh with amusement as she explained to them that she didn't mean the sleeping-in-the-woods type of cabin. This dog of the new day has her own frequent flyer miles account. You once heard that every time a bell rings, an angel gets its wings, but when flying on these wings, every time a bell rings, it's just your little angel ringing the flight attendant so she can ask for more peanuts.

Plane Truths

She's a first-class bitch all the way. When you book the reservation for your tropical vacation for two, explain to the travel agent that this is the honeymoon you two never had. While on the phone, motion to your little bitch that you are booking a first-class trip for the two of you. She will be as excited as you are.

If she meets the petite size requirements and has a pup carrier that fits under the passenger seat, you can bring her in the airplane cabin. When you squeeze her into her polka-dot rollaway carrier before boarding the plane, she may begin to question this first-class journey. But once you enter the plane and she is greeted by smiling ladies with high heels and big rings, she'll feel more at ease. She usually will be required to stay in her carrier under the seat, but there are ways around this. As you board the plane, be sure to grab one of the fleece blankets that are tucked in the overhead bins or draped across passenger seats. Once the plane takes off, unzip her bag and place her on your lap under the blanket. She will be much happier snuggled up with you than stuffed under the seat.

Tell her to keep quiet or it's all over. She will most likely weigh her options and keep a low profile. When the flight attendant asks for your drink order, request some water in a dish for your little stowaway. Make a toast to her. Try to get her to sleep. Tell the flight attendants the two of you are on a much-needed vacation. Ask if you can get a pair of wings from the captain to pin on your bitch's collar. Once the attendants realize how adorable she is, they may allow you to hold her on your lap until the plane lands.

Note: *If you're worried she may be fearful of flying, talk with her vet before the trip and get a prescription to relax her. During the flight, make sure she does not drink alcohol with her meds. Be sure to watch the movie with her or read her a story aloud. If she is scared, the sound of your voice will soothe her. Remember that as her first-class flight attendant, it is your job to make her comfortable during the plane ride.*

Join the Pile High Club

While in the air, if she starts to whine, paw at the window of her carrier, or show unusual anxiety, she may be having an emergency. She may need you to take her to the bathroom. Pick her up in her carrier and do exactly that. Place on the bathroom floor one of the absorbent square puppy pads you brought (these pads are disposable potty mats that she can go on just about anywhere), and wait for her to do her thing. When she's finished, clean up, spritz the bathroom with her favorite perfume, and stuff the dirty pad in the waste bin.

Note: *Avoid feeding her for three hours before boarding the plane. Not only will this help her avoid motion sickness, but also it lessens the chance of her having to make a number two while in the air.*

Her Puppy Passport

When jet setting, she must carry some important documents with her. Just as you can't go anywhere without proper identification, she usually won't be able to go anywhere without her health and vaccination certificates. At least two weeks before you leave for your trip, you will have to get your vet to sign a document that says she is OK to travel and in perfect health. Also, research where you are going to see if she needs shots or would need to be quarantined. Put her travel documents in a special wallet and keep it in one of the pockets of her carrier or with your own travel papers.

You can create a snazzy folder to keep her papers in for future trips. If you get a window seat on the plane, ask the passenger next to you to take a picture of you and your bitch looking out the window. When you return home from your trip, glue this picture to the front of a small folder to store her health records and all the paperwork she'll need for her next trip.

Note: *Keep handy a magazine picture of a famous dog that looks like your bitch in case the authorities give her any problems. This may also be a good opportunity to bring that portfolio you made for her (see page 33). The dog on the Caesar pack probably never had any trouble getting on any of its flights.*

Beware of Pupsicles

Pupsicles are little bitches who are stowed below the plane's passenger cabin, where the luggage is kept. If, in an emergency, the plane suddenly drops elevation, the lower cabin could freeze—and she could, too. Do not take this chance with your little bitch.

Travel to a New Level of Communication

A cold nose by any other name is still a cold nose. Teach her these basic international commands and impress the locals when you travel. Back in the States, she'll love showing off her multilingual abilities, and she'll revel in how smart all your friends say she is.

French	German	Italian
kiss, baiser	kiss, kuß	kiss, bacio
cat, chat	cat, katze	cat, gatto
dog, chien	dog, hund	dog, cane
love, amour	love, liebe	love, amore
cookie, biscuit	cookie, plätzchen	cookie, biscotto
limousine, limousine	limousine, limousine	limousine, limousine
down, descendez	down, unten sie	down, riducete
sit, asseyez	sit, sitzen sie	sit, sedete
stay, restez	stay, bleiben sie	stay, rimanete
come, venez	come, kommen sie	come, venite
fetch, prélever	fetch, holen sie	fetch, prevalete

Japanese

kiss, kisu

cat, neko

dog, inu

love, dai suki

cookie, kukki

limousine, rimugin

down, fuse

sit, osuwari

stay, mate

come, koi

fetch, tottekoi

Spanish

kiss, beso

cat, gato

dog, perro

love, amor

cookie, galetta

limousine, limusina

down, baje

sit, sientete

stay, permanezca

come, venga

fetch, traiga

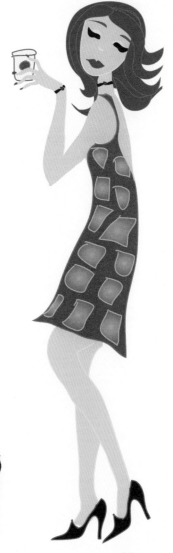

Choose a Dog-Friendly Hotel

The two of you will want to stay at a five-star hotel that welcomes her and offers all the amenities she'll need. When reserving a room, ask about the hotel's diva-dog services:

🐾 Is there a dog walker on staff?

🐾 Are any items on the room-service menu suitable for dogs?

🐾 Is the room equipped with special dog toys or beds?

🐾 Will the doorman take her out late at night if she has a potty emergency?

Also ask if celebrities often stay at the hotel. Say that the reason you're asking is that sometimes her fans become too much and you're wondering if she can use the private back entrance. Be creative. Questions like this will get the staff at the front desk gossiping and will ensure you are treated very well while staying there.

Note: *Never leave her alone in the hotel room. If you have to get a latte or do some shopping without her, see if the hotel offers a puppy au pair service or can refer you to one that's nearby.*

CHAPTER 11

Girl's Best Friend

Diamonds are overrated

Her friendship is forever. As you get down on one knee to fasten the ring on her collar, you envision your journey. Who you were before her . . . and what your life is now like with her. Contemplate how you will be different when she is gone. Your little bitch will indeed touch your life in a big way. The sparkle she will leave in your heart will far outshine any that adorns your finger. So whether you're a bitch on a budget or a rich girl, make the most of every shared moment.

She Likes to Play with Toys

You'll never forget that horrific night when you made dinner for your boyfriend's parents. As you finished dessert, your little bitch ran off with one his mother's shoes. Everyone chased the little bitch up the stairs, and she retreated to her favorite hiding place under the bed. She growled, protecting her loot, along with all the other stash she had under there. The four of you had her cornered and stuck hopeful arms under the bed in an attempt to save that $700 Manolo. Just when you thought coaxing her out by offering her a trip to the shoe store for her own pair of stilettos wasn't working, she dropped the Manolo from her jaw, and it came to rest beside her other prized possession under the bed.

"Oh my!" your beau's mother said, as his dad mumbled something about how you should probably try to rescue the shoe in private. You weren't sure why everyone was acting so weird, until your boyfriend and his parents scurried out of the room and you heard the entire family discussing the "dildo the dog had under the bed" as they trotted downstairs. It was then you realized that the hot-pink, oversized rubber dog toy you'd bought her last week, the one she'd been hoarding under the bed since you brought it home, resembled a dildo. When you returned downstairs, you knew you only had one option—to embrace your inner HMB and explain that only one bitch in the house plays with toys and it's not you.

The toys you buy her can make a big statement about who she is, not to mention who *you* are. So choose wisely. Because a spoiled bitch is never too old to play with toys, she will expect you to provide a constant supply of them, regardless of whether it's Christmas or her birthday. Not only will continually replenishing her toy stash help to entertain her should she have to play alone, but it will also keep her from eating your furniture and clothes.

Here are some toys she is sure to like. You won't be embarrassed to have any of these scattered about the next time company comes over.

❧ Plush stuffed toys and chic squeakies. Look for stylish shapes and themes, like a plush martini glass and matching squeaky olive. Squeaky steaks, old shoes, and toys that resemble road kill are not her style. Remember, she wants to be like you and live in your world.

❧ Funny-shaped rubber toys. She could spend untold hours chewing and working out the stress of her day. Get her some indestructible rubber chew toys and watch her go to town.

❧ Bubbles. Blow them in her direction and watch her chase and try to pop them.

❧ Toys that "speak" to her. If she's a talkative girl, get her some toys that speak sweet nothings to her.

❧ Pull toys. She'll love it when you use her toys to play tug-of-war with her. Rather than the tried-and-true rope toy, try to find pull toys that are more feminine, such as one shaped like cherries.

Note: *Get her a toy box with her name engraved on it. She will like having a place to keep her stash, and she will be happy that it's one you approve of.*

Wish Her a Yappy Birthday

A true party growl, she loves birthdays—especially her own. Be sure to buy her a pretty party dress for the occasion and invite all her four- and two-legged friends. Also make sure she is the first girl to secure a sparkly party hat. She loves theme events like muttini parties (cocktail attire a must) and luaus (with a tiki bar, leis, and pig ears for party favors). No matter what theme you choose, every party should have the following:

- Cute matching invitations, plates, and napkins

- Games and contests

- Treats and toy prizes for guests

- Birthday cake, complete with candles and the "Happy Birthday" sing-along

- Party favors to take home in a doggy bag

- A photographer

Calculate Her Age

Everyone knows a bitch ages differently than a girl ages. Use this guide to celebrate her milestone birthdays. She will appreciate it.

- **Her 1st (dog-year) birthday.** At just five weeks old, you may not have even met her yet. If you have, buy her a little birthday cake. Help her blow out her candle and make a wish, and let her have free reign by sticking her little paws in her cake. A small gathering should consist of close family and friends. Be sure to take a video and have everyone say something nice about her. Years later the two of you will be able to laugh at how much she has changed and how badly everybody dressed.

- **Her 13th birthday.** She becomes a teenager at just 1 year, 2 months, and 3 weeks. Throw her a party with a princess, pink, or sparkle theme.

- **Her sweet 16.** She becomes a true lady at 1 year, 6 months, and 1 week. Throw her a party featuring lacy tablecloths, frilly dog beds, and a cornucopia of sweet treats.

- **Her 18th birthday.** Though she can't drive or vote, she is legal at 1 year, 8 months, and 2 weeks. Throw her a disco-themed party that lasts all night long.

- **Her 21st birthday.** Take her on a 21 run—a tour of all your neighborhood bars—when she's 2 years old. Don't let her drink too much. She's still a novice.

- **Her 30th birthday.** At 4 years and 3 months old, she'll want a more sophisticated celebration. Throw her a Parisian party: Serve Brie and baguettes, and speak to her in French. (See page 130 for French commands and words you can teach her to impress her friends.)

- **Her 40th birthday.** When she is 6 years and 9 months old, take her on a weekend spaw getaway for just the two of you. When you return home to her "surprise party," keep her at ease while those closest to her partake in a "roast" of funny stories about her. Make sure when you are toasting with champagne you remember her significance and beauty.

- **Her 50th birthday.** At 9 years and 3 months old, it's the golden anniversary of the day she was born. Dress her in gold lamé and give her a golden sponge cake with one candle on top.

- **Her 60th birthday.** Celebrate her new senior status at 11 years and 9 months old by throwing a prom for her. Rent a band and be sure to get plenty of photos of her male mutt pals in their cute little bowties and cummerbunds.

- **Her 75th birthday.** When she's 21 years and 9 months old, throw her a cruise-theme party. Rent a shuffleboard set for the occasion.

- **Her 100th birthday.** She'll be an old girl at 14 years and 2 months old. Make a video tribute to her life using home movies and the travel photos you've taken together over the years.

Girls' Night In

What better way to remind her that she's your best friend than to throw a slumber party for just the two of you? Here are some activities she'll love:

🐾 Give each other matching pedicures. When all your paws have dried, paint your nails with a sparkly polish.

🐾 Prank call an old boyfriend who suggested she sleep on the floor. Have her pant heavily in the phone.

🐾 Rent some classic love stories and comedies on DVD (such as *Lady and the Tramp* or *Best in Show*). Make pupcorn and cuddle up on the sofa together under matching blankets.

🐾 Sleep in sleeping bags on the living room floor. Find a cable channel that's running a classic movie or Scooby Doo marathon, and leave the TV on all night.

Ten Ways to Make Her Tail Wag

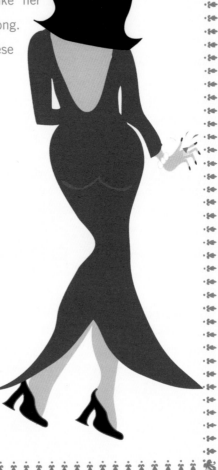

It is the little things that will make her happy and keep your relationship strong. Remember her each day in one of these special ways:

1. Sing to her.
2. Read her bedtime stories.
3. Wink at her.
4. Rub her belly.
5. Wear matching bikinis with her.
6. Garden with her.
7. Bring her flowers.
8. Pay her compliments.
9. Make her cookies.
10. Stare at her adoringly.

Read Her Sky-Candy Horoscopes

Herscopes are your destiny. She too will want to gaze at the stars with you to ponder what the future may bring. Get her a matching pair of sunglasses to read these with you, because the future for her is very bright.

Bark at the moon, swing on the stars.
Girls with big dreams drive better cars.

Aquarius

January 20 to February 18

The water is yours, lap it up

You're a rare and exotic pedigree, up to date on all the latest fashions and luxury carriers. You love the challenge of chasing tail but aren't interested in being leashed by anyone. To get ahead, try playing a good old-fashioned game of fetch in your own backyard and eating the dry kibble in your bowl. Being a minimalist may get you that slick new carrier you've been eyeing.

Pisces

February 19 to March 20

Cast your line, reel in your dreams

You have a tendency to adopt every rescue animal who comes along, but you need to learn you can't save them all. It's time to harness your overaccommodating disposition and unleash your self-indulgent spirit. You love tub time, so why not flea your responsibilities and take a dip? When you're done, put your paws up for a manicure while enjoying a soothing massage of your velvety ears and silky scruff.

Aries

March 21 to April 20

The bold and the brave sexy girls send the stars in spiral twirls

You've always dreamed of a storybook love affair. And now your moment has arrived. Just as you've been thinking, "Why didn't I get a dog sooner?" she's been wondering, "Why didn't I get a *girl* sooner?" Celebrate your devotion to each other with fresh flowers, scented candles, and homemade pasta for two. When your proverbial prince charming does come along, he'll have to love you both, or the deal's off.

Taurus

April 20 to May 20

Charge—get what you want

Ever loyal and understanding, your personalities sometimes make it difficult to tell which one of you is the dog. Instead of rolling over, take charge of your destiny: Run off for the weekend to that spaw you've been dreaming of. A little pampering will keep your tail wagging for weeks to come. You're pretty good about spending your bones on practical things, but this time the investment in yourself might be kibble better spent.

Gemini

May 21 to June 20

The sins of the twins

At the park, you're a regular dog magnet. Most of the other bitches dig you, and you handle the ones who don't with total cat-itude (feline-like aloofness). You're not afraid to embrace your inner bitch, and you enjoy behaving with wild abandon. Though your alpha tendencies may attract some pussycats, remember who you are: In the end, you like your companions to be a little alpha.

Cancer

June 21 to July 22

In a pinch, make your dreams come true

Find your favorite squeaky toy and blanket, because you're not really in the mood for the martini scene. Instead, take a bubble bath, put on your fuzzy slippers, and reread *Valley of the Dolls* together. Allow yourself to indulge in some quiet time. When you do hit the city, always bring a carrier along. There's nothing like the comfort and safety of home.

Leo

July 23 to August 22

Unleash your inner roar

You've always been somewhat of a show dog. But this year will take the prize. The spotlight is trained on you, so don't blow it. Sniff out new connections that will help you paw your way to the top. It's great that you two have each other because your tendency is to be a little self-centered and standoffish. This year is your dish, so lap it up, Leo.

Virgo

August 23 to September 22

Virgin temptress

Organize all your favorite collars, leashes, and shoes. Your preparedness will help you keep your cool when you meet that dreamy new stud. Men like this are always fascinated by your purebred (yet bad-girl) nature. If you tire of him, you'll still have her to cuddle with when he's gone. If you decide to keep him, he'll just have to get used to sleeping with both of you. Otherwise, he can be an outdoor boyfriend.

Libra

September 23 to October 22

The scales are always tipping in your favor

For someone so logical, you sure are spending a lot of time matching your collar with your leash before you go out. Your social life is sizzling, so indulge yourself. But beware of companions who've run off their leash: Although they might seem like a lot of fun at first, they always end up back at the pound. You can keep the balance you're so accustomed to by taking a girl/dog yoga class.

Scorpio

October 23 to November 21

Score everything you desire

You're a mysterious and sexy breed, Scorp. The other bitches might accuse you of attracting their studs, but it's not your fault they can't resist your scent. Still, never let things progress past friendly frolic. Your devotion to your best bitches runs deep, but if you don't start showing it you'll end up at the doggy psychologist. Don't worry, though: You can always follow the appointment with an afternoon of shoe shopping.

Sagittarius

November 22 to December 21

Aim to be a star

It's time to play, go for a run, sniff out new territory. You'll agree to wear your harness, but only if there's a thrilling adventure involved. If you're going to be spontaneous, keep it on the puppy pad. You're not one to turn up your snout at a little trouble—after all, you're an adrenaline hound. Never be afraid to bare your teeth, but try not to be so bossy. Everyone loves you already, Sag. You'll get much farther on charm.

Capricorn

December 22 to January 19

CEO of your destiny—Catch Every Opportunity

You're a well-trained breed. You have all your tricks down and you love to lap up the praise. If only you could get your paws on some playtime. The truth is you enjoy working and you're nothing less than professional. You know the secret to being sexy is intelligence. Cap, you can be trusted off your leash. In fact, you know exactly where you're headed and are terrific at leading the pack.

The Príncess and the Flea

To help her fall asleep at night, read her this bedtime story:

*Once there was an imprisoned princess
Who was rescued from her dungeon by a queen.
The royal court was not sure if the princess was really a princess
So they put one flea in her bed as a test.
The princess tossed,
And she turned,
And she itched and she scratched.
The entire night she exhausted herself in search of the flea.
In the morning the queen greeted the princess cavalierly.
The princess told the queen she had not slept a wink.
The queen smiled and said, "You are a purebred, indeed . . .
Welcome to the castle."
The princess lavished herself in a flea bath and a paw massage
And she lived happily ever after.*

About the Authors

Sister and brother **Lori Pacchiano** and **Ryan Pacchiano** founded High Maintenance Bitch, a manufacturer of sophisticated dog apparel and accessories, in 2002. With humble beginnings in their grandmother's garage, today they are considered leaders in pet fashion; their products are available in hundreds of stores worldwide and in the gift baskets for the Golden Globes. With a large fanbase that includes numerous celebrities, it is little wonder they have been featured in many magazines and newspapers and on such TV shows as *Access Hollywood*, *Dateline NBC*, *The Osbournes*, *The Simple Life*, *Today*, *Tyra*, and *The View*. Reality TV fans will also recognize Ryan as one of the cast members of Bravo's *Showdog Moms and Dads*. Both authors live in Seattle.

Michelle Goodman has written about pup culture, human mating rituals, and offbeat careers for such publications as *The Bark, Bitch, Bust, CityDog, Salon,* and the *Seattle Times*. She lives in Seattle with her 80-pound lapdog Buddy.